SUCCESSFUL ij

Successful U is a transformative guide designed to bridge the gap between spiritual faith and practical personal development. This book offers a structured roadmap for readers seeking to align their internal beliefs with external achievements.

The central theme focuses on "building success God's way," emphasizing that true well-being comes not from hustle alone, but from identity, purpose, and alignment. The structure follows a progressive journey through seven "Keys," moving from the internal foundations of belief and vision to the external manifestations of action and legacy.

SUCCESSFUL Ü

7 Keys to Success, Personal Growth, and Well-Being

"Success isn't something you chase,

it's something you become from the inside out."

Shez Nel

INWU Publishers

A subsidiary of INWU Limited

20–22 Wenlock Road

London

N1 7GU

Book Cover by INWU

1st edition 2025

This book is dedicated to my Angel
the woman who loved me when others didn't come back for me,
who opened her home, her heart, and her arms without condition,
and who showed me what strength, faith, and service truly look like.
Your love became my foundation.
Your wisdom became my compass.
Your legacy lives on in every life I touch.
To my children
You are my why, my reminder, and my greatest assignment.
Everything I've built, healed, and become was first for you —
So you would never question your worth or your place in this world.
And to every reader who has ever felt unseen, abandoned, or unworthy —

This book is for you.

You matter.

You always have.

Contents

Introduction:

My Why

There was a time when I believed I wasn't worth coming back for.

My choices, relationships, and future were shaped by these lies.

I was raised by my grandmother, who I knew loved me deeply. Yet, watching other children in her care happily go home with their parents, while no one came back for me, sowed the beginnings of unworthiness that was felt in every part of my life.

The belief that *you're not worth it* stayed with me for years. I accepted love that hurt, dropped out of college, entertained relationships that left me drained, gave loyalty to people who hadn't earned it, and numbed pain with bad habits. I was empty, stuck in a cycle I didn't know how to break.

Then came the turning point, a key moment that began to change everything. It marked the beginning of a new chapter, one that required a different approach.

I realised that prayer alone wouldn't save me.

If I wanted to break generational cycles and reshape my story, I had to move.

I had to decide: stay or rise and rebuild.

This required discipline, obedience, strategy, and a mindset shift.

I got real with God and real with myself. I took ownership of my healing. I stopped blaming my past. I wrote a new vision. I renewed my thinking. I took responsibility for my results.

It wasn't easy. But it was necessary.

Today, I woke up next to a husband who loves and honours me. I lead both a business and a charity that changes lives. I get to choose how I start my day.

I broke the cycle.

And that's what this book is about: *becoming the 'Successful U.'*

🎯 What Is "Successful U"?

"Successful U" is not about chasing a perfect life or ticking off every goal.

It's about discovering, embracing, and living as the most successful version of yourself—the one God envisioned for you before outside influences shaped your identity.

It's about **faith in action**: not standing by or waiting passively for change, but actively collaborating with God through discipline, courage, and clear intention to become your best self.

This book will help you:

- Break cycles
- Overcome fear and doubt
- Take ownership
- Produce tangible results through faith and action

It will show you how to build success authentic to you, not by the world's definition, but by an ordained vision for your life, because true success starts within.

 This Journey Will Guide You Through:

Before You Turn the Page

Take a moment to reflect:

- What did you believe as a child about yourself that you now know is not true?
- Have you been trying to prove yourself to someone or something?
- Can you forgive yourself for what you didn't know back then?

Affirmation:

"I am no longer living from my wounds. I am healing, rising, and becoming the person God always knew I could be."

☀️ What Success Really Means

We grow up believing that success is simple to attain: set a goal, work hard to achieve it, and you've made it.

But if that is true, how come so many people who the world considers to have "made it" still feel unfulfilled? Why is it that some people with money, influence, and status still wake up with a deep emptiness in their hearts?

Success has lost its true meaning.

Our culture makes success a checklist: job title, home, family, income, and popularity. Miss a box, and you feel inadequate—like you lack something or have failed—fueling disappointment that saps your confidence.

Even at respected levels, it's never enough; another ladder or milestone always appears.

Maybe you've felt that pressure too.

You might long for a cosy two-bedroom home, but social media makes you feel like you need a mansion. Even with a mansion, the next thing "V(C{ is a bigger pool or spa. The goalpost keeps moving.

Maybe you're content with a 9-5 job that provides for your family, yet society insists you should be chasing more, which can damage your peace and confidence.

I know this all too well, because I previously sought a version of success that wasn't my own.

😰 When "Success" Felt Like Suffocation

In my early twenties, I landed a high-paying job as a solicitor's secretary.

My family was proud, and my grandmother would boast to anyone who would listen about how well her eldest granddaughter was doing. They thought I had finally landed on my feet to all who looked on. My life looked successful.

Inside, I felt stifled.

I remember standing at the photocopier with tears in my eyes, buried under piles of paperwork. Every time the office phone rang, it felt like another small piece of me was dying.

I hated the work, but I stayed because I didn't want to disappoint anyone, especially my beloved grandmother. She had sacrificed so much for me.

Eventually, I found the courage to leave for a meaningful NHS role, serving people directly. Helping others I used my strengths in care and service.

It wasn't glamorous, my family didn't understand, but for the first time, I felt successful.

Later, when I became a mother, success shifted again.

It was no longer about salaries or external factors. Now, it meant being there for my son, building stability, and creating a loving home, a place where I was present, not just providing for.

That new definition didn't impress everyone.

At a family dinner, someone toasted my sibling for "making our mother proud." I sat silent, humiliated—as if raising a child alone, surviving without support, and demonstrating strength meant nothing.

Later, my aunt handed me a "Well Done" card for passing my driving test. Kind, but it felt like a bandage on a deep wound.

I went home questioning everything. Why wasn't my effort enough? Why did loving and providing for my child not count as success?

Through that pain, I found a truth that changed everything: **success is not applause; success is alignment.**

🎯 Redefining Success on Your Terms

The world offers its plan, measuring worth by income, title, possessions, or popularity. But God's definition is different.

Success isn't about the ladders you climb; it's about walking faithfully.

It isn't about comparison; it's about calling.

The mother who gains courage and leaves her corporate job to raise her children with care and purpose? That's success.

The student who sacrifices weekends to chase a dream degree? That's success.

The father who shows up every day to provide for his family? That's success.

Each of these people is progressing toward purpose. That's the real heart of success—not perfection, but *progress*; not chasing someone else's dream, but boldly living your own.

 The Cost of Chasing the Wrong Version

Pursuing someone else's version of success doesn't just drain your joy; it can destroy your health.

Nearly three-quarters of people in the UK say they've felt so stressed in the past year that they couldn't cope. In the U.S., 75% of adults report stress symptoms like anxiety, irritability, and sleep issues. Chronic stress affects the heart, mind, hormones, and immunity.

I remember coaching one of my clients. She appeared to have everything together: a great career, a beautiful relationship, and an impressive social media following.

However, as we continued through our sessions, I realised that below the surface, she was on the verge of burnout. Panic attacks, barely getting any sleep, all while she was chasing a version of success that was never truly hers.

This is what happens when we let society's definition drive us. We lose ourselves trying to become someone we were never meant to be.

It's time to stop. Choose your own definition. Choose peace over performance and purpose over pressure.

⚖️ Faith vs. the World

Here's the truth about success: the world says I can do anything if I try hard enough, but Faith says, "I can do all things *through* Christ who strengthens me."

Success in the world is motivated by self-promotion, competition, and the need to prove yourself; it seeks trophies and recognition.

Faith-based success is built on surrender; trusting that your gifts, timing, and opportunities are from God, and that you are a steward of them.

One builds ego. The other builds endurance.

One craves applause. The other produces peace.

When you align your goals with God's purpose, success stops being about *what* you achieve and becomes about *who* you're becoming.

It's no longer about striving; it's about stewarding your potential with faith and obedience.

💭 Time to Reflect

Let's pause and answer these questions honestly:

- What does success look like to *you*—beyond the world's standards?
- What expectations have you been carrying that were not yours?

- When do you feel most energetic? While chasing your dreams or when you meet others' demands?
- How has comparing affected your mental and emotional health?
- If fear of disapproval disappeared, what would you pursue today?
- What belief about success are you ready to release?

Faith in Action

- Write your personal definition of success. Make it bold, specific, and true to you, not anyone else's expectations.
- Pick one goal, big or small, and take a step toward it today.
- Practice gratitude along your journey. Celebrate the progress you've already made and the person you're becoming.

Success is not just about reaching the end destination. It's also about who you're becoming along the way as you take it step by step, one day at a time, and align your life with God's purpose.

That is real success. That is *Successful U*.

The Formula Mindset and Faith in Action

Some people believe that success is hidden away, with a secret code that only a few have access to. They look on at those who seem to "have it all" and assume they're smarter, luckier, or just more qualified than they are.

But the truth is, success isn't hidden. And it's not reserved for a select group.

Success becomes tangible when Faith and a renewed mindset work together; this is its fruit. When these two powerful forces unite, they can transform your entire life. They will break cycles, turn your mess into a message, and rewrite the chapters of your story, turning potential into actual reality.

Faith without a renewed mind often leads to procrastination, waiting for change without taking the necessary steps to prepare for it.

Having a renewed mindset without true faith often leads to burnout, where we strive endlessly without knowing our purpose and lose our peace.

Lasting transformation occurs when belief and discipline come together, and your faith guides your daily actions.

Faith Alone Is Not Enough

There was a time when I believed prayer would fix everything. I prayed for my situation to change. I prayed for my pain to end. I prayed for a better life.

And while prayer gave me strength, it wasn't until I *moved* that my life began to transform.

The Bible says, "Faith without works is dead." That's not a warning—it's an invitation: faith is active. It's not only believing God can, but also preparing for when He does.

Think of faith as the seed. It holds power and potential, but it needs soil, water, and sunlight to grow. That's where mindset comes in: the daily choices, habits, and decisions that create the environment for your faith to bear fruit.

The Power of a Renewed Mind

"For as he thinketh in his heart, so is he." (Proverbs 23:7)

Everything you will ever achieve in life begins with your mind.

Your thoughts shape your decisions. Your decisions shape your habits. And your habits shape your results.

If you believe you are unworthy, you will live beneath your potential.

If you believe success is for "other people," you will unconsciously sabotage your own.

If you believe nothing can change, you will never try.

When you renew your mind by challenging lies with truth and replacing fear with faith, you create new patterns. This builds resilience and helps you see opportunities rather than obstacles.

Mindset isn't about positive thinking or "good vibes." It's about intentional transformation, taking control of your thought life so that it aligns with God's word and His vision for you. It's about reprogramming the way you think so you can live the life you're called to live.

My Transformation Formula

My central message is this: transformation is not random. It follows a clear process—applying your faith, renewing your mindset, and taking responsibility for your choices. Lasting change happens when these steps are intentional and repeated.

1. **Renew Your Mind** – Break free from limiting beliefs and build a mindset planted in truth.
2. **Take Responsibility** – Stop blaming the past or waiting for someone to rescue you. Own your results.
3. **Set Clear Goals** – Write the vision and make it plain. Create success on your terms.
4. **Take Consistent Action** – Small daily steps build continuous momentum.
5. **Partner with God** – Trust His timing, follow His direction, and walk in obedience.

Transformation is a lifestyle, not a one-off event. Building on the last step you took, each one creates real change.

The takeaway message: intentional, consistent decisions over time lead to lasting transformation.

Lessons Learned from My Own Journey

Waiting for permission was no longer an option for me. The day I decided to follow the process, everything changed.

I began making decisions that aligned with the woman I wanted to become. I wrote clear goals rooted in God's purpose for me, not out of fear or a desire to please people.

Some days I didn't feel like showing up, but I did, and I created habits like reading, journaling, planning, and praying. I started to walk in boldness and faith.

And slowly, the outside changes began to reflect the internal ones.

Cycles were broken.

Doors were opened.

And purpose started taking place.

The truth is, transformation isn't about doing more; it's about becoming more.

Practical Faith: Where the Spiritual Meets the Strategic

The main message is simple: faith and practical action go hand in hand. Faith without works is dead, and mindset shapes the actions you take. Renewal starts in your mind.

Faith says, "God will make a way."

Mindset says, "I'm going to prepare the ground."

Faith says, "I believe God has a plan for my life."

Mindset says, "I will take the steps that align with that plan."

Faith trusts the seed will grow. Mindset tills, waters, and protects the soil. Together, they create the environment for miracles.

It's Not About Where You Start

One of the most powerful lessons I've learned is that success isn't determined by where you begin; it's defined by how you *build*.

I started my journey feeling broken, unworthy, and lost. But I chose to renew my mind, take action, believe that God had more for me, and partner with Him in creating it.

Now is your time. Make the choice today to partner with God, renew your mindset, and take your first bold step toward the life He has for you.

Don't wait, act now and begin your transformation.

It doesn't matter how many times you've failed or how far you feel from your goal. What matters is that you can choose today to think, believe, and act differently.

💭 Time to Reflect

Before you turn the page, pause and reflect:

- What limiting beliefs are holding you back right now?
- In which areas of your life have you been waiting for change without preparing for it?
- Where in your life can you take more ownership of your results?

If you want to change, the time to act is now. Choose one action that will encourage your faith. Write it down, take that step today, and commit to it.

Faith in Action

- **Renew your thoughts.** Identify one negative belief and replace it with a scripture that speaks truth over that area of your life.
- **Write the vision.** Set one clear, faith-driven goal that excites you. Break it into a small, actionable step you can take today.

Take immediate action—renew your thoughts by identifying one negative belief now and replacing it with a scripture that speaks truth over that area of your life. Set a clear, faith-driven goal that excites you and break it into a small, actionable step you can complete today. Pray specifically over that area of your life.

Write the vision. Set one clear goal, invite God into the process, ask for wisdom, strategy, and courage, and act on what He shows you.

The Power of the Mind

"Renew your mind, and God will transform your life."

Your mind is the very foundation of personal development and growth, shaping how you steer through challenges, how you see yourself, and how you approach new opportunities. It can either push you forward or hold you back.

Understanding Mindset

A **closed mindset** says, "This is just who I am" or "It won't work for me." It builds walls and resists change. And those walls keep people stuck.

I once worked with a client who dreamed of leaving their 9-5 job to pursue a buried passion. After life-changing news, they felt regret but still couldn't start. A past business failure convinced them they would fail again. Their inaction only reinforced their fear.

But let's look at the other side. A **growth-focused mindset** changes the game: it empowers you to embrace feedback, even when it stings, because you know mistakes are part of the path. It keeps you curious, adaptable, and willing to learn.

I think of another client who had never run cross-country before but wanted to do so in honour of their late mother. At first, they didn't know how to begin, but their mindset was different: "I've never done it, but I can train and learn."

Even though they lost the first race, they did not see it as a failure. Instead, they saw it as a step forward and a lesson learned.

Breaking Old Patterns

The moment I lost my beloved grandmother, I knew I needed real, lasting change. Her passing forced me into a new level of responsibility—not just for myself, but for my children. There was no one left to rescue me. It was on me now.

In the past, I'd numbed pain with distractions: alcohol, nights out, anything to avoid truth. I'd promise I was done with toxic relationships, only to return when loneliness came. I'd talk about self-love, dress up with friends, and convince myself I was healing.

Until the cycle repeated.

Why did I keep returning to what hurt me?

Because my vision was still limited. I could see a way out, but only partially. Real change meant challenging my beliefs and opening myself to new possibilities, even without all the answers.

I knew there was more to life than what I could see in front of me.

I wasn't okay, but I was ready to try. I was eager to uncover everything I had yet to become.

And in that moment, the decision to try again was the real beginning of the transformation.

🎯 The Successful U Framework: A Roadmap For Transformation

Before we go further, I want to give you the big picture—the roadmap that will guide you through this book and your transformation.

I call it the **Successful U Framework**, held up by four essential pillars. View these as vital steps that help you break old patterns, renew your mindset, and move boldly into the life you were meant to live.

1. Renew Your Mind

Transformation always starts here. You cannot build a new life with the same old thinking. Learning to replace limiting beliefs with empowering truths is the foundation of every other step.

2. Break Limiting Beliefs

Many of the barriers in your life exist only in your mind. Identifying and dismantling those beliefs is how you break cycles and step into freedom.

3. 🔨 Build Empowering Habits

Success isn't just about motivation. It is the result of daily discipline, small decisions, and consistent actions that align with who you're becoming.

4. ☝ Live on Purpose. The Goal is to live a life that you build authentically which reflects your God given purpose where faith and action work side by side.

This book will guide you through each stage. You will gain insight into the mindset shifts that enable transformation and discover practical steps to make it a reality.

 The Truth About Mindset

Your mindset is not just a thought pattern; it's a spiritual and mental foundation that shapes everything else.

It determines whether you stay stuck in the past or step into your purpose. It influences whether you see challenges as roadblocks or opportunities. And it decides whether you settle for survival or push for transformation.

Change doesn't happen by accident. It begins with a decision, a conscious choice to believe that growth is possible, that God's promises are for you, and that your future is bigger than your past.

When you align your thoughts with truth and pair faith with action, there's no limit to who you can become.

✍️Mindset In Action: Your First Step

Now we shift from inspiration to application because change happens when you act.

Action Step: Rewrite the Narrative

This is a good time to take notes and write your top three limiting beliefs you've taken on about yourself. They might sound like:

- "I'm not good enough."
- "It's too late for me."
- "People like me don't succeed."

Now, next to each one, write a new truth to replace it. These truths should reflect both who you *are* and who you're *becoming*. For example:

- "I am worthy of growth and success."
- "It's never too late to start over."

💭Time To Reflect

It may feel simple, but this is the first real step of transformation: taking your thoughts captive and speaking life where doubt once lived.

Before moving on, pause and consider:

- What beliefs have shaped the way you see yourself and your potential?
- Where have you allowed fear or past experiences to limit

your growth?

- What small actions could you begin taking today to align your mindset with truth?

🌟 Affirmation

🗒️ Over To You: Reflect & Apply

"I am free from old patterns and limiting beliefs. My mind is made new, my faith is active, and I am becoming who I was born to be."

- What do you honestly believe about your own potential for growth?
- When you see someone succeeding in an area where you've struggled, what story do you tell yourself about your ability to do the same?

🌟 Final Thoughts

Developing your mindset isn't about pretending life is easy and ignoring your challenges.

It's about believing and knowing that growth and change are possible even when the odds seem against you. It's about refusing to be defined by the pain, not denying it exists.

⛓️ Breaking the Chains: Overcoming Limiting Beliefs

"The stories you tell yourself will either build your future

or bury it."

You can own every tool, every opportunity, every ounce of potential, but if you don't believe change is possible, you'll sabotage yourself before you even start.

That's the destructive power of limiting beliefs. They don't just shape how you *think*; they shape what you *do*. And what you do determines everything.

In Chapter 1, we laid the foundation: your mindset is the soil where transformation grows. Now it's time to dig deeper: to pull up the weeds that have been choking that soil for years.

This chapter is about exposing and breaking the hidden narratives that have kept you stuck, so you can finally walk in the freedom and purpose God designed for you.

🎯When you finish this chapter, you will be able to:

- Understand what limiting beliefs are and where they come from
- Recognise how they've been shaping your decisions and your self-worth.
- Learn how to challenge, reframe, and replace them with truth.
- Take practical steps to move forward with confidence and clarity.

What Are Limiting Beliefs?

Limiting beliefs are the invisible chains that keep you tied to the same place, no matter how badly you want to move forward.

They're the thoughts, often so familiar we barely notice them, that whisper, *"You're not good enough." "It's too late." "You'll never change."*

These beliefs usually form over time. They are born from past experiences, childhood wounds, disappointments, trauma, or even other people's opinions.

Maybe someone once told you you'd never amount to anything. Perhaps a failure from years ago still echoes in your head. Maybe you've internalised society's message about what "someone like you" can or can't achieve.

Over time, these messages become part of your inner script, and that script directs the story you live.

One of my clients struggled deeply with this. She would often say, *"It's too late for me to change careers. I'm too old now, my time has passed."*

It wasn't true, but she believed it so strongly that she never applied for jobs, never learned new skills, never took risks. Her life didn't stay small because she lacked talent. It stayed small because her *beliefs* told her it had to be.

How Limiting Beliefs Take Root

Looking back on my own journey, I can see how limiting beliefs had their grip on me, too.

When I was in school, I constantly found myself in situations I wasn't emotionally equipped to handle. I was in a toxic, violent relationship during a crucial time in my education, and it consumed everything.

I'd drag myself to school after nights filled with fighting and chaos, physically and emotionally exhausted, trying to hide the bruises from my family and friends.

At the time, I thought this was love, so I stayed. My unquestioning loyalty kept me stuck.

But my studies suffered. I was unable to attend extra revision classes, which took a toll on my emotions, and this led to a lack of focus; by exam time, I was totally unprepared.

I passed a few subjects, but failed the ones I needed most. That failure dented my confidence. I started to believe that I wasn't smart enough. Perhaps education wasn't for people like me. My dream of working with children, maybe even becoming a social worker, felt entirely out of reach.

It took me years to understand what was really happening. I wasn't "bad" at school. I was traumatised, fighting battles no teenager should have to fight. And that trauma was stealing my capacity to perform.

Once I faced that truth, I could offer myself compassion. In that moment, I realised I was not a failure; my environment had made it almost impossible for me to achieve success. Seeing the truth in my situation allowed me to reject the lie that my future was doomed and that I would not flourish.

Why Limiting Beliefs Hold Us Back

Limiting beliefs don't just influence what we think; they shape what we *do*. They act like a glass ceiling, quietly convincing us that our efforts are pointless, our dreams are unrealistic, or our potential is limited. They lead us to shrink ourselves before we ever get a chance to soar.

And perhaps the most dangerous part? They're often *invisible*. We don't even realise they're there; we think we're just "being realistic." But realism, when rooted in fear, is just another form of doubt.

These beliefs become invisible chains because they change how we respond to life. The bottom line is that if you believe you're bad with money, you may never even try to save or budget because you have already told yourself you cannot do it. If you believe you are not into people, you may miss opportunities to build connections that could help you grow your business or network. And if you think it's too late, you may never take those first steps towards your dreams.

The truth is: belief shapes behaviour, and behaviour shapes results. If you want new results, you have to start with a new mindset and new beliefs.

How Growth-Focused Thinking Differs

The opposite of a limiting belief is a growth-focused perspective, the belief that with effort, learning, and perseverance, you can grow, change, and improve.

Growth thinking says, *"I'm not there yet, but I can get there."* It views failure not as evidence of inadequacy but as a stepping stone toward mastery.

Here's what that shift looks like in real life:

Limited Belief	Growth-Focused Perspective
"I can't change."	"I can learn new things, and I will improve over time."
"I'll never be good enough."	"With effort and practice, I can get better at anything."
"I don't have the skills to be successful."	"I can develop the skills I need with time and commitment."
"This is just who I am."	"I can transform any part of myself with intention and practice."
"Failure means I am not able to reach my full potential."	"Failure is a chance to grow and get better."

Limiting beliefs trap you in a cycle of self-doubt, creating stagnation.

If you have a growth-focused mindset, you will turn obstacles into opportunities and challenges into training grounds, not roadblocks.

It isn't just positive thinking. It's a powerful, practical way of approaching life that changes the trajectory of your future.

Faith in Motion

Planning with Purpose

Defining and Pursuing Your Goals – "Faith without works is dead."

Belief must be paired with action to bring about tangible results, as faith without works is dead.

Therefore, let us set our goals with purpose.

"God doesn't need you to have it all figured out. He needs you to trust Him enough to start."

Turning Growth into Goals

I used to think I was making progress simply because I was always doing something: reading books, attending workshops, and journaling early mornings. I was full of ideas and motivation.

But after a while, I started to notice something unsettling: I was busy but not fulfilled. I was growing, but not where I wanted to be.

I realised I was moving, but not in a direction. I did not have a clear goal.

Now or Never: The Moment Everything Changed

"It was now or never, and I knew it."

As a mother, I was doing everything I could to survive this thing called life. To the outside world, it looked like I had it together. I was working, raising my children, and managing a home.

But inside, I was restless. Everything I truly wanted – purpose, fulfilment, peace – all felt painfully out of reach.

It had only been a short while since the passing of my grandmother. I was still coming to terms with the traumatic labour, where I almost lost my life and my baby girl.

I was still going to work; however, it had become a burden, and a cloud hung over me. The passion I once had for it had slowly faded.

More than a decade had passed since I began my role at the NHS, where I enjoyed serving patients, but it had now left me frustrated. Deep down, I knew the time was coming for me to move on, even though they all wanted me to stay.

My grandmother always told me I was capable of more, but the question was how?

I didn't want to miss precious moments with my children while they were in childcare for long hours. I didn't want to hide or water down my faith just to fit into spaces that no longer felt aligned with it.

I felt drawn to serve, to step fully into ministry, to pour into others and be a blessing in a significant way.

I knew my purpose was evolving, and my current life could no longer contain the woman I was becoming.

Even my circle was shifting. The conversations with friends no longer resonated. Their focus was different from where I felt God was leading me.

I was grieving, disconnected, and disinterested in the life I was living. Sleep was rare; I skipped meals, and my weight was falling off me. Stuck in a cycle of existing, not living, reading every book, attending every service, yet never translating that knowledge into action.

The pain was relentless. Nightmares would tear me from my sleep, reminding me that my safe place was no longer here. Whose warm smile and comforting embrace had always made everything feel bearable was gone. She may not have been my birth mother, but she was the woman I called mother.

The one who always brought me calm in the storm, the one who knew the right words to say when my heart was overwhelmed. A home-cooked meal, a remedy for my baby, or the quiet knowing that I was never alone; she was always there, but now she was gone forever.

I was grieving, desperate for change and a renewed purpose. My career was not a fit. My old ways were not serving me. My faith was still there, but I was struggling to move forward.

I had reached a crossroads: continue existing in the safety of the familiar, unfulfilled, uninspired, and disconnected, or step into the unknown and pursue the life I knew God called me to live.

The question that haunted me was simple but powerful: What now?

I found myself stuck in a familiar place. On one hand, there was a place I could stay that was familiar and safe, but on the other hand, I knew there was an endless array of new possibilities available to me if I took a leap of faith into the unknown.

The choice was mine: stay stuck in survival mode or dare to dream.

And even though I felt unqualified, unprepared, and unsure of the path ahead, something deep inside whispered, Start anyway.

If I was ever going to change my life, it had to begin with one decision: the decision to stop talking about change and start building it.

My Wake Up Call: The Day I Wrote It Down

The moment I asked myself, *what now?* Something shifted.

I realised no one would hand me change, and that confidence wouldn't just appear. It would require action—even small steps.

I stopped waiting for the perfect scenario, ideal plan, or time.

When I asked myself, *What now?*, I realised change wouldn't come wrapped in clarity, but would require action—even if small.

I stopped waiting for the perfect version of me and knew I had to move forward.

A Realisation

A few years ago, after one particularly exhausting season of going in circles, I had a realisation.

I had just finished a course on personal development, and I felt inspired, having come away with insight and pages of notes, fuelled with fresh ideas. I felt hopeful this would be the moment I would see change.

To my surprise, within a month, I was facing the same frustrations and feeling stuck.

One night, as I flipped through my journal, I was confronted with a question that stopped me cold: *What exactly am I working toward?*

I stared at the page, but I didn't have an answer.

That realisation broke something open in me. If I couldn't define the destination, how could I ever expect to get there?

Writing It Down

So I turned to a blank page and did something I had never done before: I wrote it down.

I wrote about the life I wanted (not about the pain I experienced) five years into the future without hesitation, without shrinking, and without worrying about how it would happen.

For the first time, I gave myself permission to dream.

That night, I built a vision that I could break down into tangible, smaller actions.

Making the decision to take what was floating around in my mind and write it down on paper brought my hopes and dreams to life.

Within six months, that vision began to bear fruit. I rebuilt my morning routine. I aligned my daily choices with the woman I knew I was becoming.

The shift wasn't dramatic or instant, but it was real. And for the first time in a long time, I felt momentum pulling me forward.

Breakthrough: Faith in Action

I decided to hand in my notice; my stomach was full of knots, I had butterflies, nervous, but determined.

Trembling as I typed my resignation letter, doubts were creeping into my mind. Voices that questioned my worth reappeared, screaming all at once.

Are you being foolish? How can you walk out of a solid job? Are you delusional? It's safe here. You know everyone, and they love you. Staying here meant a job for life.

At least there, I wouldn't fail.

But deep down, I knew staying would be the ultimate betrayal not to my employer, but to myself. I had outgrown the woman who played small; it was time to run my own company.

The still, quiet voice inside me kept whispering, *Trust. Move now.* There was no more room for fear.

So I went straight into unemployment, uncertainty, and faith.

I didn't have a backup plan. I didn't know what was waiting for me on the other side. But one thing I knew with absolute clarity: I couldn't stay.

It happened almost suddenly. As soon as I took that step of faith, things shifted.

It all felt as if I was watching someone else's life. Imagine this was the same girl who once believed she would never be enough, now building real, lasting impact.

Every small step showed me that I had made the right choice, reminding me of my beloved grandmother, the woman who had sacrificed so much for me.

I prayed and hoped she was proud that everything she had sown into me was not in vain. Though she wasn't here to witness the complete transformation, I carried her wisdom into every meeting, every decision, and every courageous "yes" to the next step.

It was in that season I learned a life-changing truth: all the praying, dreaming, and planning in the world mean nothing if you never move.

And so I did something that terrified me: I chose action.

When I handed in my resignation, my managers pleaded with me to reconsider. With tears in their eyes, they reminded me how loyal and dependable I had been, how much we'd overcome and done together.

And while that meant a lot, this time I had to choose loyalty to something bigger - to myself, to my children, and to the vision God had planted in my heart.

It was time to sow into *me*.

And once I did, everything changed.

With the weight of that old chapter lifted, I had the clarity and capacity to focus on the woman I was becoming.

My personal life transformed in ways I never saw coming. Within less than a year, I was married, something that had once felt impossibly far away. From single to standing at the altar happened faster than I could have scripted it myself: three months of courting, followed by planning the wedding of my dreams with over 400 people in attendance.

But I didn't stop there.

I enrolled in a course that stretched me, equipping me with the skills and confidence to redirect my career completely. Suddenly, I was signing contracts, viewing potential office spaces, and sitting across from people whom I was now hiring.

At the same time, I fully stepped into ministry and launched a non-profit organisation dedicated to supporting the homeless, families in poverty, and vulnerable youth.

Life became full of long nights, early mornings, and countless sacrifices, but it was a different kind of full. I woke every morning with gratitude, and my heart was whole. I poured every ounce of energy into something that mattered deeply to me.

The joy of living in line with my purpose is something words could never truly explain. A small idea scribbled in my journal became a vision and a reality far beyond what I could ever imagine.

And when people ask me how I did it, how I went from merely existing to truly thriving, my answer is always the same:

First, I believed.

Then, I took action.

Because belief alone is powerful. But faith with action—that's where transformation begins.

Growth Is Not Enough Without Direction

Growth is a powerful beginning, but it's not the only destination.

You may have read all the books, attended every seminar, and collected endless pearls of wisdom, but if that growth doesn't have direction, it becomes action without any true meaning. Change for the sake of change will only keep you going around in circles.

It's not enough to *believe* things can be different; you have to define what "different" actually looks like for you.

Where is this growth leading you? What are you building toward?

Without that clarity, even your best intentions can leave you stuck, busy, and unfulfilled.

True success isn't about how many boxes you tick off or how many goals you achieve. It's about building a life that intentionally aligns with who you truly are, one that reflects your values and honours your purpose, allowing your light to shine from the inside out.

Clarity begins with vision. And vision isn't just a dream or a wish—it's the blueprint that keeps you grounded when distractions try to take you off track. It's the *why* behind everything you do.

When the road gets tough, or doubt starts to creep in, your vision is what reminds you why you started and where you're going.

So don't just chase growth—give your growth direction.

Write your vision clearly, make it plain. Define your purpose boldly. And let that purpose guide every step forward.

🎯 The Vision to Action Plan

From Intention to Impact

Growth without direction is like running on a treadmill; you're moving, but you're not going anywhere.

You've acknowledged any issues, done the inner work, the mindset work. Now it's time to build something with it.

This is where we shift from dreaming to doing. From vision to action. From intention to impact.

I call this process the **Vision to Action Plan™**, a simple yet powerful framework designed to help you clarify where you're going and map out the exact steps to get you there.

🧭 Step 1: Clarify the Vision – "Your Why"

Your personal vision isn't just a good idea; it's your roadmap.

It's the anchor you'll come back to when distractions arise, and everything feels disarrayed, when self-doubt creeps in, and the journey feels too overwhelming.

Before you write a single goal, you need to define *why* you're on this path.

Over to you to reflect and answer these questions:

Integrity matters.

🤫 Don't rush this part. Take a moment to be still.

Find a quiet space to sit with these questions and allow your answers to come naturally, flowing from a deeper part of who you are.

🎯 Step 2: Set Goals That Actually Work

Once you're clear on your vision, let's give it structure.

Goals are how dreams become reality, but not just *any* goals.

Vague, half-finished ideas like "I want to be successful" or "I'll get healthier" won't change your life. Clear, measurable, action-able goals will.

That's where the **SMART Method** comes in as a proven system to bring structure to your vision:

- **Specific:** Define exactly what you want.
- **Measurable:** Decide how you'll track your progress.
- **Achievable:** Choose goals that will stretch you but are still realistic.
- **Relevant:** Align them with your bigger overarching vision.
- **Time-bound:** Give them a deadline.

⚡ Step 3: Tighten Goals into Actionable Ones

Loose Goal: "I want to read more."

❌ No plan.
❌ No way to measure progress.
❌ No timeframe.
❌ No deeper motivation.

SMART Goal:

"I will read for 20 minutes every morning for the next 30 days to build a daily habit that supports my personal and professional growth."

The difference is night and day. One is a wish, the other is a plan.

Try it again with a different example:

Loose Goal: "I want to be better at accepting feedback."

SMART Goal: "I will ask for specific feedback from my manager and one colleague after each project for the next three months so that I am able to make improvements through reflection and learning."

See the shift? It's focused. It's actionable. And it's *trackable.*

Step 4: Align Goals With Your Core Values

Not every goal deserves your energy.

Before committing to anything, ask yourself:

- Does this support the person I want to become?
- Am I chasing this out of faith or out of fear?
- Will this move me closer to peace or further from it?

Goals rooted in your core values—faith, family, growth, freedom, and purpose—will sustain you when motivation runs low. These are the goals worth building your life around.

Step 5: Activate Your Vision

Time to make it real.

Now is the time to bridge the gap between your *intentions* and your *actions*. Use the space below to turn ideas into movement.

Practical Exercise:

1. Write your 5-year vision on one page, and describe your life in detail: Job. Relationships. Health. Habits and Spiritual Life.
2. Set 3 SMART goals for the next 12 months that directly align with that vision.
3. Break each goal into 6-month milestones.
4. For each milestone, write 2–3 action steps you'll begin *this month*.

Remember: You don't need to figure out every detail today. Just keep moving and take the next step in faith.

✨ Final Thoughts: Faith. Vision. Action.

Having a vision doesn't mean you'll control every outcome; it means you trust the process even when you can't see the whole picture.

It's believing that what you feel stirring inside you is real and worth pursuing, even if the path isn't easily accessible.

A growth mindset can thrive and will not just sit around waiting. It's not just an idea—it's a tool, a weapon, and a calling.

But none of it will matter if it never leaves your head.

Purpose without a plan is just potential.

And potential without action? It changes nothing.

At some point, you have to stop waiting for the perfect conditions and decide that what you have in your hands is enough to start today, you are sufficient.

The dream that's been tugging at your heart isn't going to build itself. The future you desire isn't going to just turn up at your door. You have to *go after it.*

⏰ The Power of Now

The truth is: transformation doesn't happen "someday somewhere." It happens the moment you choose to stop existing and start building.

It shows up in the next decision you make, the email you send, the conversation you initiate, the step you take *today*.

Too many people waste their lives in a state of limbo, "waiting for when I'm ready." But readiness isn't a feeling; it's a choice.

And the most powerful thing you can do for your future is to move *before* you feel completely prepared.

Your assignment isn't to figure out every detail of how. It's about taking the next faithful step one day at a time with what you have and where you are, and trusting that the rest will unfold in time.

So write the vision. Make it plain. Build the plan. Then *execute*.

Because building the life you desire isn't found in the safety net of staying still; it's created in motion.

And every small, courageous step forward is proof that the story isn't over yet. It is your moment. It is your chapter.

Don't wait for "one day." Today is the day.

Resilience and Adaptability

"Do not judge me by my success, judge me by how many times I fell down and got back up again."

- Nelson Mandela

The Power of Rising Again

Now that we've seen how limiting beliefs hold us back, it's time to learn how to *rise*.

Resilience bridges who you were and who you're becoming. It's the quiet strength whispering, *"I'm not finished yet,"* when all feels broken.

Healing from trauma and loss builds a strength forged by experience, not books. Real resilience isn't pretending everything is fine; it's showing up when nothing makes sense. Resilience appears when faith outweighs fear.

For me, resilience began with one choice: to believe my present would not dictate my future. Even through tears, laughter would return. After the darkest night, joy would rise at dawn.

Hope became my anchor.

Life moves in seasons, sun follows rain, warmth follows winter. Pain doesn't last. We can't control when seasons change, but we can choose how we respond while we wait.

Every time life breaks you down, you face a choice: to remain trapped in what was, or to trust that what's coming will be better. When you choose to believe that change is still possible, you begin to heal. Victory always begins with belief — belief that healing is possible, and that no weapon formed against you can stop what God has ordained.

The Power of Resilience

If I had allowed the pain of my past to define me, I would still be living in survival mode, trapped in the identity of a victim instead of walking in victory.

If I had let the abuse I endured shape my future, I would have missed the love story written with my name on it. I would have missed *him*, the man God handpicked for me.

If I had accepted the label "college dropout" as my truth, I would have never dared to open my business, launch my charity, or serve my community in ways that impact lives today.

But I chose differently.

I chose to believe I could become more — that my pain could produce purpose. That I could love differently, live differently, and mother differently.

And I did.

Resilience isn't about having all the answers. It's about making one decision over and over again to keep going. It's about trusting that your story isn't over, even when the page feels blank.

"You may not control all the events that happen to you, but you can decide not to be reduced by them."

— Maya Angelou

Resilience Is Adaptation

Resilience isn't just bouncing back; it's adapting—learning to live when life looks nothing like you'd planned.

Setbacks often change your direction, but they don't cancel your destiny.

When trauma interrupted my education, I thought I had failed. I believed the version of me that couldn't finish school was the end of my story. But resilience showed me that the person I was *becoming* mattered more than the one I had been.

I didn't rebuild confidence overnight. It took steady steps—new routines, speaking kindly to myself, and refusing to tie my worth to my past.

It's about moving forward in a different way. Resilience taught me that it's not about going back.

Resilience is a muscle. The more we use it, the stronger it becomes.

Like physical strength, emotional resilience grows through consistent use. You build it every time you choose to rise after disappointment, to believe again after heartbreak, and to stand when you could have stayed down.

I didn't become resilient overnight. At first, I was fragile, plagued by memories of domestic violence, failed exams, and missed opportunities. Guilt weighed heavily, making me doubt myself.

But one day at a time, I learned that healing doesn't come from our perfection; it comes through our persistence.

Resilience strengthens self-belief. It teaches you that you *can* recover, rebuild, and rise again.

I still remember standing outside the college doors, hands trembling as I debated whether I should turn back. The voice of fear whispered, *"You'll never make it."*

But another voice, the quieter one, standing in faith, said three simple but powerful words, *"Just walk in."*

I walked in.

And that simple act of courage planted a seed.

Even though my time there was short, it taught me something that changed my life: when you keep going, even without certainty, miracles meet you halfway.

The Truth About Pain

One of the biggest misconceptions about resilience is that strong people don't feel pain. That couldn't be further from the truth.

Resilience doesn't mean you're not affected by pain; it means you continue on pushing through it.

It means:

- You cry and still show up.
- You doubt and still try again.
- You hurt and still hope.

Resilience is not the absence of fear; it's the presence of courage.

It's standing in the storm and saying, *"Even if I'm scared, I'll move anyway."*

Rising After the Fall: Building Resilience Through Loss

Grief has a way of stopping time.

Unless you've faced loss yourself, it's impossible to describe how heavy absence can feel. One day, the person you love is right there, breathing, laughing, and the next, there's just silence. You reach for the phone, only to remember there's no one on the other end anymore.

When I lost my beloved Angel, my grandmother; My world collapsed. The ground beneath me shifted. She wasn't just family; she was my anchor, my confidant. Losing her was like losing the air in my lungs.

The nights were long and quiet. The mornings felt endless. Grief seeped into every part of my life until even the simplest things—eating, working, smiling—felt like impossible tasks. There were moments I questioned whether I would ever feel whole again.

Work no longer mattered. My future felt lifeless. For a while, I just existed, not living, trapped between fond memories and emptiness.

But even in that darkness, something small and fragile started to grow: the will to rise again.

Healing Begins in Surrender

Because here's the truth—**healing doesn't begin in a moment of strength. It begins in surrender.**

It starts when you say, "God, I can't do this without You."

It starts when you stop running from your pain and start walking through it, trusting that somehow, one step at a time, you will see the light and joy return.

That was the beginning of my resilience story. Not a loud comeback, but a quiet return to hope.

From Surviving to Thriving

In the early days of healing, I was simply surviving—breathing, crying, repeating.

But over time, resilience shifted my focus.

It moved me from "just making it through" to asking, "What can I make of this?"

That one question changed my perspective.

I began taking what felt like broken pieces and rebuilding. The charity I later founded to serve the homeless, families in crisis, and youth without support was born from her memory. What she poured into me didn't die with her. It multiplied.

Resilience turned my grief into purpose.

And that's what resilience truly is: the bridge between heart-break and hope. It's what happens when you stop asking "Why me?" And start asking "What now?"

The Science of Resilience: Your Brain on Hope

Resilience isn't just emotional or spiritual; it's physical too.

Every time you rise after a setback, your brain is learning.

That "bounce back" moment? It's actually your brain rewiring itself through a process called **neuroplasticity**—the ability to form new pathways based on what you think and do repeatedly.

When you pray instead of panic, reflect instead of react, or ask for help instead of shutting down, you're literally training your brain to be stronger.

Research shows that resilient people have:

- More activity in the **prefrontal cortex** (responsible for reasoning, focus, and emotional control).
- Less reactivity in the **amygdala** (which triggers fear and stress).

The result? They recover faster, think clearly, and stay grounded in the face of challenges.

Resilience doesn't mean the storm stops; it means your brain and your faith learn to navigate it.

"Resilience isn't being unaffected by pain; it's training your mind and spirit to rise again."

Resilience Through Faith and Mindset

We are told in the Bible that we find strength in God through our trials; while suffering produces endurance and hope, we may be afflicted, but we are not crushed.

Spiritual resilience is an exchange of our weakness for God's unwavering strength. Ultimately, it's trusting God.

From a spiritual perspective, resilience is a divine exchange of your weakness for God's strength. It's trusting that even when everything feels out of control, you're being held by something greater.

Faith doesn't eliminate pain; it transforms it. It turns heartbreak into healing and obstacles into opportunities.

Scripture reminds us that "the testing of your faith produces perseverance", and that "those who hope in the Lord will renew their strength. They will soar on wings like eagles".

This kind of faith-fueled resilience isn't about being unbreakable; it's about knowing that when you break, God can rebuild you stronger.

Mindset is vital too.

Neuroscience tells us that your thoughts shape your resilience. Faith tells us that your focus shapes your future. Combine the two, and you create an unstoppable force: a renewed mind grounded in divine purpose.

So whether you strengthen your resilience through prayer, journaling, therapy, or small, consistent steps, the goal remains the same: to rise higher, think clearer, and trust deeper.

💡 My Takeaway: What Resilience Taught Me

Looking back, resilience became one of my greatest teachers. It showed me that my past could shape me, but not define me. It reminded me that broken things can be rebuilt, that ashes can birth beauty.

Resilience taught me that I didn't need to have everything figured out to move forward. I just needed to take the next faithful step.

This chapter of life isn't about perfection; it's about perseverance. It's about believing that even when a page feels closed, God is still writing.

Every setback became a setup for a greater comeback.

And though I've walked through shadows, the sun always returned.

Resilience grounded in faith is courage in action. Even when you can't see the full picture, you believe that God can restore you.

💭 Time To Reflect

This would be a good time to make notes.

Reflection Questions to Cultivate Deeper Resilience

1. When facing challenges, what helps you find the strength to keep going?

(Prayer? Scripture? Talking with a trusted friend?)

2. How do your beliefs — whether spiritual, personal, or both — support your resilience?

(Do you rely on faith in God? Core values? Or a personal mission statement you are committed to?)

3. What habits do you practice that help you cope with setbacks?

(Journaling, affirmations, rest, reframing negative thoughts?)

4. Can you recall a time when a difficult experience led to unexpected growth?

(A job loss that led to new opportunities, or a heartbreak that brought healing?)

5. How can you maintain and build your hope and positivity when life feels overwhelming?

(Gratitude, worship, meditation, speaking truth over fear?)

6. How have your past struggles contributed to the way you approach challenges today?

(Are you more patient, wise, or compassionate because of them?)

✅ Action Steps

🙏 **Ground Yourself Daily:** Practice gratitude or prayer to reconnect with peace and thankfulness.

🎯 **Start Small:** Choose one simple, achievable goal when facing a challenge.

🔄 **Reframe:** When fear or negativity creeps up, ask, “What can I learn from this?”

🤝 **Connect:** Lean on people who support you — mentors, friends, family, community.

🎉 **Celebrate Progress:** Every small victory is proof that you’re growing stronger.

Resilience is not just about bouncing back; it's about becoming a new version of yourself, rising up after each setback, refusing to give up, learning the lessons, and growing from them.

It's choosing faith over fear, growth over grief, and purpose over pain.

You don't need to have all the answers, just the courage to keep moving.

Keep turning the page, keep choosing hope, and keep believing that the shore is closer than you think.

Because no matter what you've faced, you are still here.

And still you rise.

Health And Well-Being

The Foundation Of Success

🚨 When My Body Forced Me To Listen

For a long time, I told myself I was fine.

I was slim, active, and always busy. From the outside, I looked healthy—but my body was telling a different story.

I was running on a mix of responsibility and adrenaline. I was a supportive wife and present mother, navigating my daughters' teenage years and a son at university.

I was building a business, leading a ministry, running a charity, delivering food parcels, counselling others, and showing up wherever needed.

I felt happy to be reliable for others and to show up strong. It was something I always needed growing up, but rarely had outside my grandma.

But in meeting **everyone else's needs, I was neglecting my own well-being.**

Then came the health scare. Hospital appointments. Tests. Waiting rooms. Biopsies. Moments where your mind is all over the place and your body can't keep up.

I sat and thought about school runs, responsibilities, and those who depended on me. Then I asked myself: **What would success mean if I wasn't here to reap its benefits?**

That question changed everything.

 The Wake-Up Call I Didn't See Coming

Even though I looked "healthy," I wasn't heart-healthy.

My diet had slipped without me realising it. Meals became fast food between meetings or takeaways after long days, sometimes skipped entirely because there was "no time."

I made sure everyone ate well, but I ran on empty myself.

Low energy became my normal. Stress felt constant. And as I entered a new chapter of my life, hormonal changes started to add another layer I couldn't ignore.

My body wasn't failing me. It was *protecting* me.

So I paused, and I listened.

I sought professional advice about my health. I changed my diet, adding more vegetables, more fruit, and real nourishment.

Being slim does not guarantee true health.

And more importantly, I learned something even greater:

Rest is not laziness.

Balance is not selfish.

And slowing down is not failure.

🔄 The Reset: Putting Me Back Into The Plan

That season forced a reset.

Not just physically, but mentally and emotionally too.

I had to confront a hard truth: I couldn't pour from an empty cup. I had to stop treating my well-being as an afterthought.

Yes, I still had goals and purpose, and I was called to serve. However, God never asked me to destroy myself in the process.

There are seasons to work and seasons to rest. There are times to give and times to be refilled.

I had been anxious, overwhelmed, carrying concerns about my children, responsibilities, and calling, trying to manage alone.

And that's when I realised:

Burnout doesn't arrive suddenly. It whispers first.

Fatigue. Irritability. Disconnection from your body. Ignoring warning signs because "others need you."

I chose to disrupt that pattern.

I slowed down. I took stock of my mental and physical health. I learned to say no without guilt.

And I gave myself permission to be human and step down from trying to be the hero.

💡 What This Season Taught Me About Real Success

Success isn't only an achievement. It's about sustaining achievement with well-being.

Without health, success is unstable and won't last. Purpose without balance is risky. Achievement without well-being is short-lived.

That health scare didn't deter my journey; it **protected** it, allowing me to become aware.

It reminded me that:

- My body is not expendable.
- My needs matter.
- My presence is more valuable than my productivity.

Let this chapter remind you: Prioritise your well-being now, so your body doesn't force you to.

Because taking care of yourself and using wisdom isn't stepping away from your purpose.

It's actually being a good steward over it.

Health Is Not a Detour

Your physical, mental, and emotional health are deeply connected.

Chronic stress weakens the immune system, impairs concentration, disrupts sleep, and impairs emotional regulation. When one area suffers, they all eventually follow.

There is no easy one-time 'fix' for your health. It's something you maintain over time.

Success without well-being cannot last.

A Pattern I See Too Often

I once worked with a woman who reminded me a lot of who I used to be.

She was capable, organised, and deeply committed to everyone around her. She showed up for her family, her job, and her community without hesitation. On paper, she was doing well. But her body was telling a different story.

She came to me exhausted. Not tired, *drained*. She talked about headaches she'd learned to ignore, constant digestive issues, and a level of anxiety she'd normalised as "just life." Like many people, she believed slowing down meant falling behind.

What struck me most wasn't how much she was doing but how little space she had left for herself.

As we talked, it became clear that her idea of strength was rooted in endurance. She believed rest had to be earned and that taking care of herself would somehow let others down. However, her body was already letting her know all was not well.

The changes didn't happen overnight. It started when she decided to make one decision: to stop treating her well-being as an option rather than a necessity.

She didn't give up on her life. She didn't abandon her responsibilities. She simply learned to pace herself, nourish her body properly, and set boundaries without guilt.

Months later, she told me something that stayed with me:

"I didn't realise how much I was surviving until I finally started living."

That's the quiet danger of neglecting your health: you don't always notice it happening. Until your body forces the conversation.

This Isn't Just a Personal Story, It's a Pattern

What others and I have experienced isn't rare.

In the UK, **around 74% of adults report feeling so stressed in the past year that they felt overwhelmed or unable to cope** (Mental Health Foundation).

In the United States, studies show that **over 80% of workers report job-related stress**, with stress linked to fatigue, anxiety, poor sleep, and long-term health issues.

In other words, many of us are functioning, but not at our best.

Chronic stress doesn't always announce itself dramatically. Sometimes it looks like productivity. Like responsibility. Like "just getting on with it." But over time, that pressure shows up in the body—in energy levels, digestion, immunity, hormones, and emotional resilience.

Burnout Is Not a Badge of Honour

What strikes me is this:

Most people don't burn out because they're weak; they burn out because they deeply care.

They care about their families. Their work. Their calling. Their purpose.

But without boundaries, care turns into depletion.

I realised I needed balance, not perfection, not withdrawal, just balance.

🔄 The Reset Decision

Before you turn the page, pause.

Not to think.

Not to analyse.

But to decide.

Because there comes a moment in every transformation where information is no longer enough. Inspiration won't carry you any further. Another chapter won't change what a decision will.

This is that moment.

Somewhere along the way, many of us learned how to keep going while slowly falling apart. We learned how to show up, perform, serve, and succeed, all while ignoring the quiet signals our bodies, minds, and hearts were giving us.

Resilience doesn't mean running until you collapse.

Success does not mean grinding yourself into the ground.

And strength doesn't mean sacrificing yourself to prove a point or by playing the martyr.

Sometimes the bravest thing you can do is just stop... and reset.

Your Reset Starts Here

I want you to choose **one** area of your health that you've been neglecting.

Not all of them.

Not a complete overhaul.

Just one.

Ask yourself honestly:

- What has my body or mind been trying to tell me that I've been too busy to hear?
- Where have I been pushing through when I should have been paying attention?
- What is one boundary I need to set to support my well-being?

Now decide:

What is one small but intentional change I will make this week?

It could be:

- Booking a health check you've been putting off
- Choosing nutritious meals instead of surviving on unhealthy ones
- Going to bed earlier and getting the rest you so desperately need
- Saying no to one thing that drains you
- Taking a real pause without guilt

Whatever it is, write it down.

Being clear about our intentions creates commitment.

Read This Slowly

This is not you quitting.

This is you choosing sustainability.

This is not a weakness.

This is wisdom.

This is not selfishness.

This is stewardship.

You are not behind in needing rest.

You are not failing for needing care.

You are not less committed because you're choosing to protect yourself.

You are choosing to stay well and finish what you started.

The Truth You're Allowed to Live By

You don't need to earn rest.

You don't need permission to slow down.

And you don't need to break yourself to prove your worth.

So today, let this be the line drawn in the sand.

The moment you stopped surviving on empty and started choosing to live fully, wisely, and well.

This is your reset moment: choose to prioritise well-being for real, lasting success.

And everything that comes next will be stronger because of it.

Remember, awareness creates choice.

And choice creates change.

Your health is not in the way of your purpose.

It is the foundation that enables you to fulfil it.

 Health Is The Strategy

The Strong Body. The Focused Mind. The Grounded Soul.

🎯 The Holistic Life Advantage™ Framework

Success isn't just about what you accomplish in life.

It's about who you become along the way.

Goals can be reached at the cost of exhaustion.

Titles can be worn while feeling burned out.

Milestones may come while you're silently struggling.

And that's not success, that's survival parading as progress.

That's why health and well-being are not optional extras on this journey called life.

They are the foundation.

In this chapter, I want to introduce you to what I call **The Holistic-Life Advantage™,** a simple yet powerful framework that ensures your success is sustainable, not just impressive.

The truth is: you don't rise *above* your health.

You rise *to the level of it.*

The Holistic-Life Advantage™ rests on three pillars:

- **The Body** — your physical foundation
- **The Mind** — your focus and clarity
- **The Soul** — your emotional and inner self

When these three work together, resilience and well-being arise naturally, strengthening each other rather than working in isolation.

💪 Pillar 1: The Body Is Your Foundation For Everything

Your body is the vehicle that carries your purpose.

Ignore your body, and it slows or stops you. When I pushed forward, ignoring signals, my body almost halted.

I had to realise that caring for my physical health doesn't mean going to extreme lengths.

It simply calls for consistency.

The Big Three

These non-negotiables are not for perfection, but for progression:

Movement

Exercise isn't a punishment; it's permission to operate at your best.

Walking. Strength training. Stretching.

The goal isn't about high intensity; it's more about consistency.

Fuel

What you eat is important.

Whole foods. A balanced diet. Staying well hydrated.

This may seem restrictive, but it's about respect for your body.

Rest

Sleep is where the recovery process truly happens.

It sharpens thinking, stabilises your mood, and protects your health.

Aim for 7–9 hours, not as a treat, but as discipline.

Action Step: Build Your Physical Foundation

This week, commit to:

- **Movement:** One activity you enjoy, 3–4 times
- **Fuel:** Plan one full day of nourishing meals
- **Rest:** Choose a consistent bedtime and stick to it

Consistent small habits beat big plans done occasionally.

🧠 Pillar 2: The Mind — Protecting Your Focus

You can't build a powerful life with a constantly overwhelmed mind.

Mental well-being isn't about eliminating stress — it's about learning how to respond to it.

Unchecked stress leads to burnout, poor decisions, and emotional exhaustion.

Regulating your mind creates a space for clarity, creativity, and calm confidence.

One of the simplest, most powerful practices is **intentional stillness**.

Prayer. Journaling. Quiet reflection. Reading.

Moments for your mind to breathe and exhale.

I practice this daily to cultivate peace and prepare for the day. If I miss this time, my mood shifts and overwhelm clouds my thoughts. These moments are precious and never taken for granted.

Action Step: Daily Mental Reset

For the next 7 days:

- Set aside **5–10 minutes** daily.
- Sit quietly, breathe deeply, pray, or journal.
- When your mind wanders, gently bring it back.

This isn't wasted time; it's mental maintenance.

Your emotions don't make you weak.

Ignoring them is a weakness.

Emotional well-being means learning how to feel without being ruled by feelings.

It's about self-compassion, honesty, and a healthy expression of your needs.

Remember, self-care isn't selfish; it allows you to love others in a healthy way while loving yourself.

It's stewardship.

Neglecting your emotional needs causes resentment, fatigue, and disconnection; it leaves you unable to love and truly care for others.

Action Step: Emotional Refuel

This week, choose **one activity** that nourishes you emotionally:

- Reading
- Creating
- Being around people with whom you feel safe
- Resting without allowing guilt to rob you of your peace

Put it in your calendar.

Protect it as you would an important appointment, because it is.

The Mind Body Connection

Your health systems don't operate alone; they work together.

Chronic stress weakens your immune system. Poor sleep raises anxiety. Unprocessed emotions, when buried, can drain physical energy.

That's why **The Holistic Life Advantage™** unites the body, mind, and soul; each pillar relies on and reinforces the others.

Action Step: One Daily Alignment Practice

Each day this week:

- Do **one activity** that supports both body and mind

Example:

- A walk followed by deep breathing
- Stretching paired with prayer
- Exercise followed by journaling

Alignment builds the momentum needed for consistency.

🌟 Final Takeaway:

Health Isn't A Phase, It's A Strategy

Health is not something you fix and leave. I built it into my habits; now I can't imagine my life without it.

It's something you *honour* as you build.

Prioritise body, mind, and soul to ensure your success.

You don't need to pile it on and do it all at once. You just need to start choosing yourself consistently.

Because the strongest version of you? That's the one who endures until the end and finishes well.

What One Action Will You Implement Today?

Write it down.

Commit to it.

Let's go!

Resources:

Appendix A: 30-Day Health and Wellbeing Tracker

Develop Positive Relationships

Support your growth through the right people.

No person is an island.

Whether in the UK or the US, human connection is more than a nicety; it's essential for thriving. Recent findings show that loneliness is a profound threat comparable to smoking 15 cigarettes a day affecting mental and physical health even impacting performance in schools and workplaces according to *U.S. Surgeon General's Advisory(2023)*.

We are living in a time where loneliness has quietly become a global health crisis. A 2025 report revealed that one in six people worldwide now experience chronic loneliness—causing over 871,000 preventable deaths each year and elevating human connection from a personal desire to a public health necessity. Yet, hope lives in the same data. Decades of research on adult development consistently show that the single greatest predictor of a long, happy, and healthy life is not wealth, status, or achievement but the presence of strong, positive relationships.

Positive relationships with spouses, family, friends, mentors, and even acquaintances serve as the foundation of a meaningful and fulfilling life. They give us a sense of peace and belonging, enhance our joy, and become our anchors during tough times.

But not all relationships are created equal. Some lift us. At the same time, others may weigh us down.

In this chapter, we'll explore how to develop intentional **relationships that nourish and support your growth** while also learning how to **protect your energy from those who don't.**

📖You'll learn how to:

- Recognise the value of authentic connection
- Communicate in ways that build trust
- Set healthy boundaries
- Resolve conflict with clarity and compassion
- Ultimately, create a circle that reflects the best version of you

💫 The Importance of Connection

Humans were created for connection with others. From the moment we are born, we seek out relationships with people who make us feel safe, seen, and understood.

Even the Bible says it's not good for man to be alone. God created us to work together and to lift each other, two is better than one. He said, "Love others as we love ourselves, support the weak, and do good to others."

A community is key to a well-rounded life. It's not about quantity, but rather the quality of the relationships you have in your life, as they not only support your emotional needs but also take a toll on your mental and physical health.

Studies show that people with strong social support systems are:

- More resilient to stress
- Less prone to depression and anxiety
- More likely to achieve their goals
- Live longer, healthier lives

🧠 Key Mental Health Benefits of Positive Relationships:

Beyond the science, there's something even more profound at play: **growth is enhanced when we are around others who believe in us.**

Key Mental Health Benefits of Positive Relationships:

1. **Emotional Support**: Positive relationships offer a safe space for sharing emotions, reducing feelings of isolation or loneliness.

2. **Increased Self-Esteem**: When surrounded by supportive people, individuals feel valued, which boosts self-worth and confidence.

3. **Resilience:** Good relationships can help us bounce back from challenges. Knowing you have people to turn to in times of stress or hardship makes a significant difference in

mental resilience.

4. **Lower Stress Levels:** Positive social connections reduce the physiological impact of stress and anxiety by promoting relaxation and emotional balance.

5. **Improved Cognitive Functioning:** Positive relationships promote mental clarity and focus, which contribute to better problem-solving and decision-making.

When I started my journey toward personal and spiritual growth, I realised that my success wasn't just about what I knew or what I achieved, it was about **who I allowed into my life**. I had friendships and work colleagues who drained my energy and others who inspired and encouraged me.

The moment I decided to **invest in relationships that supported my growth** and set boundaries with those that didn't changed my life for the better almost immediately.

I sought out people who were on the same journey as myself to become the best version of themselves:

- Those who wanted to thrive and not just survive
- Who were open to change and took accountability
- Willing to make sacrifices and not make excuses for their toxic behaviour

I felt more focused, confident, and motivated once I had let go of toxic friends who chose to stay stuck, unwilling to let go of a closed mindset. I learned that the people I decided to surround myself with either pushed me forward or held me back.

As the Bible says, stay away from idle people and choose your friends wisely; these are among the first steps to building successful relationships that help you thrive in your purpose.

📖 The Story of Barnabas and Paul

Looking back at the story of Barnabas, a man in the Bible who is known for becoming Paul's advocate. He was his mentor. He was patient, taking time to encourage and support him, recognising his actual value and potential, and advocating for him to the apostles in Jerusalem, as he was a new convert.

Because of his violent past and reputation, they were afraid of him.

This relationship demonstrates to us the importance of being intentional in your relationships, not just getting comfortable, but creating a safe space for yourself and others to grow and transform.

By investing in Paul, he helped shape one of the most prominent men in early Christianity, and they both went on the first mission trip to spread the gospel in Asia and Cyprus.

This story shows us that healthy relationships are built on intention, allowing us to lift others, creating a safe space for growth and mutual success, not allowing them to remain stagnant in survival mode, but to thrive to their fullest potential, even if that means being honest and saying things that may be difficult to receive.

🤝 Build Your Support Network

Take a look at your relationships. Who brings you peace? Who inspires you? Who listens without judgment?

Start small:

- Reach out to one person today and connect with someone who is aligned with the person you are becoming.
- Express appreciation and gratitude for their friendship.
- Send an encouraging message to show support or book a coffee date to meet up in person.

Relationships need nurturing; they will not sustain themselves. Don't wait for a crisis or an emergency to lean on others; build your support network now while things are stable.

Too often, we wait for dire circumstances to arise before we reach out and make contact, always too busy or putting it off until another time. But the truth is, we make time and prioritise what's important to us.

💬 Effective Communication equals Healthy Relationships

Healthy relationships are not just sustained through love or loyalty; they also require open, transparent communication to succeed.

Think about the last time you had a disagreement and felt misunderstood. It may have created conflict or confusion. Now think of a time when you felt truly valued, and someone took the time to understand and hear you. That moment would have deepened your trust and brought you both closer.

Communication is more than just talking to someone.
It's:

- Listening with empathy to understand and not just defend
- Expressing yourself with clarity
- Being present and authentic in your interactions

Communicating well will create an environment of trust and emotional safety, setting the foundation for your relationships to flourish.

Active listening is commonly overlooked. People often listen passively, distracted and not fully engaged.

 Practice Active Listening

The next time you're in a conversation, try this:

- Put your phone away
- Make eye contact
- Repeat back what you've heard to show understanding
- Ask thoughtful follow-up questions to show you were actively listening

You'll be amazed at how quickly relationships deepen when people feel genuinely heard.

 Boundaries: Protecting Your Energy

Relationships can shape your success both positively and negatively.

One of the most potent forms of self-respect is setting boundaries.

Boundaries are not walls to keep people out; they are bridges that allow the right kind of relationships to thrive. They define what is OK and what is not OK in your interactions with others. This is vital in any healthy relationship, as people can only treat you the way you allow them to.

Very often, we feel guilty when it's time to set boundaries. We start to think about the after effects and how they could upset those we care about or make us seem selfish.

This was me. I was not always confident when setting boundaries. I used to hold back, thinking it was my responsibility to "keep the peace." But I learned that being honest with myself and others created a deeper bond and a more genuine relationship.

Let's be honest, no matter how willing we are, we **cannot pour from an empty cup.** If we neglect ourselves, we end up feeling drained and overwhelmed.

That's why I make sure to practice being kind to myself first daily, whether it's through a quiet walk, journaling, or taking a moment just to be. When you nurture yourself, you naturally attract healthier, happier relationships.

If you don't protect your energy, no one else will.

Healthy relationships begin with YOU. Understand your values, needs, and limits. Setting clear boundaries isn't about pushing people away; it's about communicating what you need to feel respected and valued and allow you to show up fully, without resentment or exhaustion.

Boundaries preserve your peace and make room for the right people to connect with you authentically. The Bible says we should love others as we love ourselves. Remember, when you honour yourself and your needs, you lay the foundation for all the amazing relationships meant for you.

Set One Boundary

Identify one area of your life where you feel overextended or disrespected. Ask yourself:

- What do I need in this situation?
- What am I no longer willing to tolerate?

Then take one small, clear step to communicate that boundary, whether it's declining an invitation, limiting time with a toxic person, or asking for support.

Boundaries are not about control; they're about clarity and respect for yourself and for others. Setting clear expectations for all involved.

 Navigating Differences with Grace

Even the best relationships will experience conflict at some point. It's not the conflict itself that destroys relationships, but how we navigate through it.

When handled well, disagreements become an opportunity for us to:

- Understand different perspectives
- Build and strengthen trust
- Clarify expectations

Even though Paul and Barnabas travelled together on missions and were close, they still faced challenges and strongly disagreed over whether John Mark should join them on a missionary trip. Their conflict was so intense that they decided to go their separate ways. Paul went with Silas, and Barnabas went with John Mark.

This clearly shows that you can disagree, but if handled with grace and understanding, there need not be any slandering; they did not attack each other. Later, Paul even spoke respectfully of both Barnabas and Mark.

Sometimes it's OK to part ways without becoming enemies.

Respect can remain intact even when plans change, and people grow apart. There are seasons, and sometimes those seasons must change.

If it is not handled correctly, it can lead to disconnection, resentment, and emotional pain.

The key is to approach conflict with curiosity, seeking the root cause and understanding what the other person is truly saying, rather than with defensiveness or combativeness. Ask questions. Stay open and grounded. Active listening more than speaking will reduce the likelihood of further misunderstandings.

We should not want to win the argument, but instead reach a mutual understanding and resolve it.

Conflict Resolution

Think of a recent or ongoing conflict and try this tactic:

1. Take a moment to breathe and pause before reacting.
2. Use "I" statements instead of blaming and pointing fingers (e.g., "I feel unheard when..." Instead of "You never listen!").
3. Acknowledge the other person's perspective and feelings, even if you disagree.
4. Focus on solutions, not who's right or wrong.

With practice, you'll learn that conflict isn't the end of the relationship; on the contrary, it can lead to deeper understanding.

🌱 Your Circle Is Your Soil

Just as a plant cannot grow in contaminated soil, you cannot thrive in toxic relationships.

The people you surround yourself with either nurture your growth or stunt it.

As you evolve, so will your relationships. Some may fall away. Others will deepen. And new ones aligned with who you're becoming will emerge.

Relationships are shaping our success both positively and negatively.

The right relationships will sharpen you and challenge you constantly to do better, not just telling you what you want to hear, but telling you what is needed for your growth. They will not be repelled by hard times; that's when they show up even more.

The key is to choose your friends wisely; the wrong relationships can lead you to ruin, but the right ones will stick closer than a brother.

Purpose and Integrity

Living True When It Costs You

Living with purpose and integrity means letting your values guide your actions, especially when tempted to compromise. It is about choosing authenticity over external gain and remaining true to yourself, even if others would choose an easier, more profitable path.

Purpose without integrity is empty.

Integrity without purpose can feel like you don't know your direction.

But when the two walk together, they create a life that feels grounded, honest, and whole.

This chapter explains how living with both purpose and integrity creates deep fulfilment, especially when tested.

🌱 Where My Sense of Purpose Began

Long before I understood purpose as a concept, I lived it.

I was always the one helping and checking in, making sure no one felt forgotten, driven partly by my own experience of feeling stuck, abandoned, or unsupported.

I was raised by my grandmother while both of my parents chose not to raise me. That absence shaped me in ways I didn't fully understand at the time. When your needs aren't consistently met as a child, you often grow up becoming the person you once needed.

I became the nurturer, encourager, and emotional anchor—roles I filled both instinctively and out of necessity.

The encourager.

The emotional anchor.

I became the "mother" of the group, not by choice but by instinct and the needs around me.

I built community wherever I went. Not always family by blood, but family by circumstance. Many of us were tied together by shared wounds: abandonment, instability, the feeling of being overlooked or unwanted.

In those spaces, showing up for others felt natural. It felt necessary.

Helping wasn't something I did to be seen.

It was something I did to make sure no one else felt unseen.

✨ What Faith Didn't Change and What It Refined

When I stepped into my faith journey and gave my life to God, serving others didn't suddenly appear; it deepened and became even more meaningful.

Encouragement, support, guidance—these were already a part of who I was. Faith didn't replace my identity; it refined it. It gave language and direction to what had always been in my heart.

I had witnessed this kind of life up close long before I ever understood it spiritually.

My grandmother's house was rarely quiet. Neighbours knocked for sugar, for advice, for help with children they struggled to raise. Sometimes they came just to sit and talk. Sometimes they came broken. At times lost.

Her table, always full, became a gathering place where needs were met and spirits lifted. With her door always open, neighbours found a safe haven and a listening ear. She gave freely because kindness was her default, not for recognition or applause.

So when I began supporting my brothers and sisters in faith, it wasn't a new role. It was a continuation of what I had seen my entire life.

 When Values Are Tested by the World

As I grew older, I began to notice something that unsettled me.

I saw people chase success at any cost. I watched them bend morals, sometimes sacrificing family and watering down beliefs.

Some traded presence for position, prioritising advancement over genuine connection. All in pursuit of money, recognition, or status.

It went against everything in me.

For a long time, I had a complicated relationship with money. Not because I didn't want it, but because I associated it with selfishness. Outside of my grandmother, many of the examples I'd seen were ruthless, disconnected, and empty. I saw people who seemed to have everything yet lacked peace.

So I made a quiet promise to myself:

No amount of success would cost me my values.

Work would never come before my children. I would never sacrifice presence for status. Money would never replace integrity.

That promise, rooted deeply in my values, shaped my choices as I followed what mattered most.

Even when high-paying opportunities came, I said no. Not because I wasn't capable, but because that required a version of me I didn't want to become.

Family always came first.

💪 Integrity Isn't Anti-Success — It's Anti-Sellout

For years, I believed that staying true meant staying small.

But life taught me something deeper: integrity doesn't mean rejecting success, it means redefining it.

Today, I live comfortably. We have an income that supports my family, helps others, and runs a charity that serves people who are often overlooked.

I no longer see money as selfish when it's used with the intention of benefiting others, not just the self.

However, everything changed with balance.

But the core never shifted.

When actions fail to align with your values, even a win can feel like a loss.

I would rather struggle honestly than succeed by selling out.

They can take opportunities.

They can take resources.

They can take comfort.

But they cannot take your character.

And a good name, a clear conscience, is worth more than gold and silver.s

🎯 Purpose Isn't What You Do, It's Why You Do It

Many people chase purpose through titles, platforms, or productivity. But purpose isn't found in how busy you are; it's revealed in what pulls at your heart when no one is watching.

For me, purpose has always looked like this:

- Helping people move forward
- Encouraging growth
- Sitting with people in the uncomfortable middle
- Getting them unstuck

That's what energises me. That's what lights me up.

Now I get to live that out fully as a qualified coach, mentor, leader, and servant. Not because I planned it perfectly, but because I stayed aligned.

Purpose doesn't always shout.

It whispers over and over until you listen.

🔑 Why Integrity Matters More Than Ever

Integrity is what keeps you grounded when success accelerates.

Without it, growth becomes dangerous. Influence becomes hollow. Achievement becomes exhausting.

Integrity asks:

- Does this decision reflect who I truly am?
- Am I acting from conviction or comparison?
- Would I still choose this if no one applauded it?

With integrity, life doesn't break. You don't have to remember who you were every time you enter a different room. You move with consistency, clarity, and peace.

Peace is the quiet reward of alignment, which is the fruit of living with integrity.

Time To Reflect: Discovering Your Why

Purpose begins with honesty.

Take a moment and write freely, no editing, no overthinking.

- What genuinely excites you?
- What problems do you feel drawn to help solve?
- What would you do even if no one paid you or praised you?

Now ask:

- How do my current goals reflect what matters most to me?
- Where am I living out of pressure instead of purpose?

Your "why" doesn't need to impress anyone.

It just needs to be true.

As you reflect, it's important to be honest: Where have you drifted from your values?

Integrity isn't about perfection. It's about awareness.

Reflect on a time you compromised your values:

- What led you there?
- What did it cost you emotionally, mentally, spiritually?
- What boundary could you set now to prevent that from happening again?

Clarity brings growth, not shame.

🌍 Living Aligned in a World That Rewards Compromise

You will be tested.

There will be moments when cutting corners looks easier. When staying quiet feels safer. When compromising seems like the quickest way forward.

But alignment offers you a long-term reward that shortcuts never do: **peace**.

When you live in alignment, you don't have to perform.

You don't have to prove anything.

You don't have to pretend.

You get to be uniquely you.

Final Reflection

Purpose gives your life direction.

Integrity gives it depth.

When the two walk together, you build a life that doesn't just look successful—it feels right on the inside.

And that kind of life?

That's the true reward: a life connected to purpose and integrity.

Closing Exercise: The Alignment Tracker

Write answers to the following:

1. What are my top five values right now?
2. Where in my life am I honouring them?
3. Where am I ignoring them?
4. What is one decision I need to make to realign?
5. What would my life look like in a year if I lived fully aligned?

Take your time.

This isn't about changing everything overnight.

It's about choosing integrity today and letting purpose unfold from there.

Financial Independence

Financial independence is choosing how you live, controlling your time and decisions.

This chapter reframes your view of financial independence. It is not just about accumulating wealth; financial independence is also about managing your time and choices.

This chapter demonstrates that financial independence is attainable.

With wise planning and consistent action, you can achieve it. Success comes from making money work for you, not just earning more.

Benefits of financial independence

Financial independence reduces stress, gives you the freedom to pursue your passions, and lets you live on your terms.

Whether you want to work part-time, travel, or start new projects, it's all possible.

🧠 The Psychology of Money: What We Believe Shapes What We Build

Money is rarely just about money.

It's about what we saw.

What we absorbed.

What we learned to associate with safety, power, love, or loss.

Before earning money, we form subtle, emotional, and often unconscious beliefs that shape how we earn, spend, save, avoid, or pursue money.

For a long time, my relationship with money was complicated. Not because I didn't want it, but because of what it seemed to cost.

What I Learned About Money Growing Up

I watched people sacrifice everything for money growing up.

- Family time.
- Presence.
- Values.
- Peace.

Outside of my grandmother, who gave generously but lived simply, many of the adults around me were consumed by the pursuit of more. More status. Recognition. Proof they had "made it" in some way."

The price they paid was often high.

- Children were left to raise themselves.
- Marriages were left strained or even broken.
- People became cold, defensive, and disconnected.

Money didn't look like freedom to me.

It looked like pressure, absence, and compromise.

So without ever consciously deciding it, I built an internal belief:

Money makes people selfish.

Success costs you your soul.

And choosing wealth means choosing to be absent.

Those beliefs came from observation and shaped my choices for years.

When Money Becomes an Internal Conflict

Because of those early impressions, I didn't just avoid greed, I avoided ambition.

I subconsciously distanced myself from money because I didn't want to replicate what I'd seen. I equated earning more with *being less*: less present, less kind, less grounded.

I told myself:

- Family mattered more than finances.

- Being integral mattered more to me than income.
- Love meant more than status.

And those things were true.

But what I didn't realise at first was this:

I had confused money itself with the ways others chose to misuse it.

That confusion began to limit my options.

When money is framed as "bad," you don't just steer clear of greed; you're also rejecting your personal growth.

You turn down opportunities not because they're wrong, but because they feel unsafe.

You equate struggle with virtue and ease with guilt.

And eventually, that belief begins to work against the very values you're trying to protect.

How Beliefs About Money Shape Our Behaviour

The psychology of money isn't about numbers. It's about meaning.

If you believe money is:

- **Dangerous** → you may avoid earning or managing it.

- **Scarce** → you may hoard or panic-spend.
- **A measure of worth** → you may overwork or compare constantly.
- **The root of evil** → you may self-sabotage when success arrives.

I didn't chase money, but I also didn't trust it.

What I later learned is this:

Money doesn't corrupt character.

It reveals it.

The Shift: Redefining What Money Is For

The turning point for me wasn't earning more; it was *rethinking why*.

I began to ask different questions:

- What if money could be a tool, not a threat?
- What if earning well didn't mean forsaking my values?
- What if financial stability actually *protected* my family rather than harmed it?

Slowly, my mindset shifted.

I realised that money in the hands of someone with integrity can become:

- Security for their children
- Freedom to choose being present over pressure

- A resource to help others
- A way to build impact, and not the ego

I didn't want wealth for the love of money or status. I realised that **money alone was not the root of all evil, but the love of it was.**

I wanted breathing room. The ability to give without fear.

That distinction changed everything.

When Awareness Replaces Avoidance

As my beliefs changed, so did my behaviour.

I stopped seeing money in only two ways, something to reject or obsess over, and began to see it as something to steward.

I learned that:

- Earning honestly is not selfish.
- Providing well is not a betrayal of loved ones.
- Wanting stability does not mean wanting excess.

Now, I live with balance.

I earn enough to live comfortably, where supporting my family is no issue, and have an overflow to help others and run a charity that serves people in need.

Money no longer competes with my values; it supports them.

And that's the difference between chasing wealth and **aligning**

it with your vision.

Why This Matters for You

Know it or not, your beliefs about money are already shaping your life.

The question is: *are they helping you or silently hindering you?*

If you grew up seeing money mishandled, weaponised, or idolised, it's natural to recoil from it.

But avoidance isn't healing. Awareness is.

Realising that you don't have to choose between:

- Integrity **or** income
- Purpose **or** provision
- Faith **or** financial growth

Reflection: Renewing Your Money Story

Take a moment and reflect honestly:

- What did money represent in your childhood?
- What behaviours around money did you witness?
- What unspoken rules did you adopt because of that?
- How might those beliefs be limiting you today?

Now ask:

- What would a healthy relationship with money look like for *me*?

- How could money support my values rather than sabotage them?

You don't need to become someone else to grow financially. You just need to become more honest about what you believe and why.

Remember, money doesn't change who you are. It amplifies who you already are.

When your foundation is built on integrity, money begins to multiply for good, not as a test for you to fail.

And when your values lead, wealth is no longer your master and does not cost you your soul. It simply gives you more leverage.

Financial Literacy

Before pursuing financial independence, you must grasp core financial literacy concepts.

Financial literacy means making informed choices about earning, managing, and investing money. Knowledge helps you control your finances and work toward financial freedom.

Here are the essentials everyone should master.

1. Budgeting: The Foundation of Financial Health

Budgeting is the first step to financial independence. It entails planning your income to cover expenses, save, and invest.

Without a budget, you risk overspending, creating debt, and

delaying goals.

I used to manage money in my mind, going back and forth between bills and shopping. Without a budget, I fell behind on bills and lost track of spending.

Using a budget changed my finances by showing me where my money went so I could make better decisions.

You can use a method that divides income into:

- **50% for needs** (housing, utilities, groceries, travel)
- **30% for wants** (entertainment, eating out, holidays)
- **20% for savings and debt repayment** (retirement savings, emergency fund, debt)

Using this method will allow you to better track spending and make adjustments as needed.

Let's now discuss the next essential steps.

Saving creates a safety net for peace of mind and handling unexpected expenses. Emergency funds, as well as short- and long-term savings, are key to financial independence.

It's wise to have an emergency fund that can cover you for up to 3-6 months so that you do not build credit or loan debts during tough times.

2. Investing: Growing Your Wealth

Having savings is important, but investing is how you create passive income and build long-term wealth.

To achieve financial independence, you need to learn how to make your money work for you. Simply saving isn't enough.

I used to think saving alone would build wealth—watching my bank balance grow—until I needed that money. Then I realized the interest wasn't growing fast enough to reach my goals.

That's why investing, which grows your money over time through compound interest, is essential.

Compound interest means your money grows over time, because you earn returns not just on what you invest, but also on the returns you've already earned. Your money starts **working for you**.

This concept is important for new investors because it shows why starting early and staying invested matter more than trying to time the market.

3. How Compound Interest Works

When you invest, you may earn interest, dividends, or growth. Leaving these returns invested adds to your original amount. Future returns are then based on this larger total.

Over time:

- Your investment grows slowly at first.
- Growth accelerates as returns are earned on previous returns.
- The longer you stay invested, the stronger the effect.

This is known as the **compounding effect**.

Example

Imagine you invest **£5,000** in a stock investment that earns an average of **6% per year**.

- **After 1 year:** £5,000 grows to £5,300
- **After 5 years:** Your investment is worth about £6,691
- **After 20 years:** Your investment grows to around £16,035

You see how it works? You didn't even have to add any extra money; the increase comes from compound growth over time.

4. Regular Investing and Compounding

Compound interest becomes even more powerful when you combine it with your **regular monthly investing**, which is very common in the UK.

People do this through:

- Stocks & Shares ISAs
- Workplace pensions
- Personal pensions (SIPPs)

For example, if you invest **£200 per month** and your investment earns an average 6% return each year for 25 years, your investments could grow to over £130,000. This is possible because your earnings are reinvested and compound over time, meaning even small regular investments can become significant.

The Importance of Time (Not Timing)

Many new investors worry about finding the 'right time,' but the evidence shows that staying invested over time is usually more important than trying to predict market highs and lows.

Starting earlier allows:

- More time for returns to compound
- Smaller contributions grow into larger amounts over time
- Less pressure to chase high-risk investments later on

Compound Interest and Inflation

In the UK, inflation means that money loses value over time. Investing lets your money grow faster than inflation, which can protect and increase your wealth.

Compound growth is one of the main ways investors aim to keep up with rising living costs.

Compounding Works Both Ways

While compound interest helps investors grow wealth, it is important to be aware that it can work against you with:

- Credit cards
- Personal loans
- Overdrafts

Interest on debt compounds just as it does for investments. That's why high-interest debt can rapidly grow out of control if not managed.

Key Takeaway for New Investors

Compound interest rewards:

- Starting early
- Investing regularly
- Staying invested for the long term

You don't need large sums of money or expert knowledge to start investing. Patience and consistency matter most for successful investing.

Setting Financial Goals

Financial independence takes planning and commitment. Setting specific financial goals is essential.

For example, saving for a new car, a holiday, or paying off credit card debt can all be included in your short-term goals.

Long-term goals might include building a retirement fund, buying a home, or aiming for financial independence by a certain age. Write down your vision, and create a roadmap to track your progress.

The Power of Passive Income: Making Money Work for You

A key part of financial independence is **passive income**, which is money you receive regularly without constant effort. This could be rental income, dividends, or royalties from a book or album.

Why is passive income so important? It allows you to separate your time from your income. Instead of trading hours for money, passive income streams create revenue that continues to flow in, even when you're not actively working.

Below is a list of examples.

Examples of Passive Income:

- **Investing in Dividend Stocks:** These pay you a portion of a company's profits regularly (quarterly or annually).
- **Real Estate:** Rental properties can generate steady income.
- **Creating Digital Products:** Books, courses, and software can be sold repeatedly with little ongoing work.

Through **peer-to-peer lending**, you can also earn interest by lending your money directly to other people or small businesses, rather than putting it in a bank.

In simple terms:

- You lend money
- The borrower pays you back over time
- You earn interest for lending your money

This is usually done through an **Online platform** that matches lenders with borrowers and handles repayments.

Instead of a bank lending £1,000, you and others might each lend a small amount. The borrower repays the loan in monthly installments, and you receive interest as income.

A partner is about saving together and taking turns; peer-to-peer lending is investing by lending and earning interest. My grandmother did a similar thing with other Caribbeans from the Windrush generation when excluded from mainstream banks.

How Financial Independence Supports a Holistic Life

Financial independence means building a life where you control your time, reduce stress, and pursue your passions.

When you become financially independent, you are no longer tied to a job out of duty or need. This opens the door to so many possibilities:

- **Less Stress:** Financial freedom provides peace of mind, knowing that your basic needs are met, and you have a safety net in times of emergency.
- **More Freedom:** This creates opportunities to pursue what excites you, whether that's traveling, starting a new business, focusing on your family, or hobbies without financial restrictions.
- **Time for Personal Growth:** Without financial stress, you can invest in yourself, learning new skills, deepening relationships, or volunteering in your community.

Achieving financial independence gives you the freedom to live your life however you want. It's a holistic approach that goes beyond money; it's about building a life that aligns with your values.

Practical Exercises

Exercise 1: Budgeting Your Way to Financial Indepen-

dence

Creating a personal budget is the first step toward taking control of your finances. Use the following steps to track your income, set spending limits, and make conscious decisions about how you use your money.

1. **Track Your Income:** Write down all your sources of income (salary, side jobs, investments, etc.).
2. **List Your Expenses:** Include rent, utilities, groceries, transportation, entertainment, and any other regular expenses.
3. **Apply the 50/30/20 Rule:** Allocate your income into the three categories: 50% needs, 30% wants, 20% savings.
4. **Evaluate and Adjust:** Review your spending habits to identify unnecessary expenses and reduce them. Can you cut back on dining out or cancel subscriptions you don't use?

Exercise 2: Investment 101 – Start Thinking Long-Term

Start by understanding the basics of investing. While it may seem overwhelming at first, it's easier than you think once you break it down. Here's an introduction to get you started:

1. **Start with Low-Cost Index Funds:** These funds let you invest in a diverse range of stocks, thereby reducing risk.
2. **Learn About Compound Interest:** The earlier you start, the more time your money has to grow. You can generate additional earnings on your investments through compound interest.

3. **Define what you want to achieve by creating investment goals.** For example: "I want to grow my investment portfolio to £100,000 by the time I retire at age 60."
4. **Invest Regularly:** Even small, consistent investments can compound over time. Commit to contributing to your investment account each month, no matter how small.

Conclusion: Embrace Financial Independence as You Plan Your Way to Freedom

Many think they have to be mean to themselves along the journey to achieving financial independence; however, it does not have to mean living without joy or denying yourself small pleasures.

Instead, it means creating a plan that allows you to live life on your own terms. By doing the work and learning financial literacy, investing strategically, and developing passive income streams, you can reduce your financial stress, create more freedom, and gain control over your future.

Whenever your stewardship journey starts remember: Financial independence is not an overnight process, but each step, no matter how small, will bring you closer to the life you truly desire.

Examples of Financial Independence

The examples shared in this chapter are provided for educational and illustrative purposes. Some scenarios are fictional or composite examples designed to demonstrate financial principles and behavioral patterns. They do not represent specific individuals, and results will vary depending on individual circumstances. This content is not intended as financial advice.

Budgeting: The Foundation of Financial Health

Sarah, 28, works in marketing. Despite a stable salary, she lived paycheck to paycheck with no savings.

She began budgeting using the 50/30/20 rule to take control of her finances.

Income: £4,500/month (after taxes)

- **50% Needs:** £2,250 (rent, utilities, groceries, insurance, travel)
- **30% Wants:** £1,350 (eating out, entertainment, shopping)
- **20% Savings/Debt Repayment:** £900 (into savings, emergency fund, and debt repayment)

With her new budgeting habit, Sarah adjusted her spending. Realising she overspent on entertainment and eating out, a plan was made to cut back and redirect those funds into her emergency fund and retirement savings.

After three months, she was amazed by her progress, having saved £2,700, which gave her much-needed peace of mind.

Saving: Building Your Financial Cushion

James is 35 years old and works as a freelance graphic designer. Although his income is inconsistent, he understands the importance of having an emergency fund.

In one of his goal-setting sessions, he set a goal to save £6,000, covering three months of living expenses, in case of unforeseen circumstances or emergencies.

- **Monthly Expenses:** £2,000 (living costs, utilities, food, insurance, etc.)
- **Goal:** Save £6,000 to cover three months of expenses

James decided to automate his savings by setting up a monthly direct deposit of £500 into a high-yield savings account.

Within 12 months, to his delight, he reached his goal. Having this emergency fund allowed James to take on projects he was passionate about without worry or stress. When his income was inconsistent, he knew he had a financial safety net.

Investing: Growing Your Wealth

Lily's investment strategy shows how consistent investing can help build wealth.

Lily is a 25-year-old, living in the US who recently started investing. She was not trying to get rich quickly but wanted to grow her wealth over time.

In her sessions, she discussed her options, and decided to start by investing in low-cost index funds and setting up a Roth (Individual Retirement Account) IRA for retirement.

- **Investment Account:** Roth IRA
- **Monthly Investment:** $3,500

Her focus is on keeping her investments diversified and low-cost.

Lily aims to save enough to retire comfortably by her early 60s. Through her dedication to regular contributions, she is leveraging compound interest to grow her wealth.

After 5 years, Lily has done amazingly well: her portfolio has grown to over $335,000 USD, and she's now well on her way to achieving her long-term retirement goal.

Beyond investing, generating passive income can further accelerate your path to financial independence.

Conclusion: Realising Financial Independence in Action

These illustrative examples show how financial independence is possible for those willing to put in the effort, make informed decisions, and stay consistent.

Whether your journey leads to budgeting, saving, investing, or building passive income streams, I have learned that every small action brings you closer to your goal of financial freedom.

A Final Word

Becoming Who You Were Always Meant to Be

Divine intervention - Renew Your Mind Transform Your Life

If you've made it this far, know this: you did not arrive here by accident.

It was not a coincidence.

Something in you was stirring long before you turned the first page. A hunger for more. A quiet knowing that the life you were meant to live requires intention, courage, and faith in action.

Just as I did not stumble into healing, you did not stumble into these pages. You sensed there must be a deeper peace, stronger alignment, greater purpose.

That knowing was the beginning of your becoming.

This book was never meant to impress you. It was meant to challenge old patterns, inherited definitions of success that were never yours to carry, and cycles of survival that now limit you.

Becoming the *Successful U* isn't about proving your worth; It's about accepting your worth.

Belief without movement stays dormant.

Action without faith burns out.

But when Faith and action move together true transformation begins.

Success isn't about recognition; it's about alignment.

Our trust in God fuels our efforts, and our efforts reflect our trust in God.

You don't need to have every step figured out. You never did. You just need the courage to take the next one, trusting that God will meet you there as He always does.

So don't close this book and wait for "someday."

Start today.

Become aligned.

Become intentional.

Become healed.

Every step forward is intentional.

As you move forward continue building a life that reflects your values and vision.

Become the best version of yourself

Become Successful U

Commit to the Lord whatever you do, and he will establish your plans. Proverbs 16:3 (NIV)

God bless,

Shez

My Commitment to Growth

A Lifelong Commitment to Learning

To solidify your commitment to growth, I invite you to take action now: complete one final exercise to support your growth.

Write a commitment letter to yourself. Do not worry about perfection or pressure—focus on growth. Clearly state what you are choosing from this day on, the mindset you are releasing, the habits you are building, and the version of yourself you are stepping into.

Sign and date your letter to mark this moment as your decision to take charge instead of drifting.

As you reflect on your journey, remember that growth, as you've learned, is not a one-time event.

Growth is a lifestyle. You may revisit these pages and exercises, refining what works and releasing what doesn't. Growth evolves as you do.

Today, I choose to stop living from old wounds and start living from truth.

I commit to:

- Intentionally growing and not passively
- Aligning my actions with my values
- Honouring my faith with discipline and boldness
- Taking responsibility for my own healing and results

- Becoming the most authentic version of myself

I release:

- Every old label that no longer defines me
- Fear disguised as comfort
- Approval seeking that keeps me small and stuck
- Definitions of success that don't align with my calling

I choose growth not once, but every day.

Signed: ______________________________

Date: ______________________________

Acknowledgments

The journey to growth is never a result of just your own, and this book exists because of the people who stood beside me, sometimes quietly, sometimes firmly, when I was becoming.

First and foremost, I thank God, whose grace met me in my brokenness and whose guidance carried me when I didn't have the strength to carry myself. Every page of this book is rooted in His faithfulness.

To my husband, my best friend, thank you for loving me with patience, covering me with support, and believing in the vision even before it was fully birthed. Your steadfastness has been a gift.

To my children, thank you for your understanding during the long days, early mornings, and late nights. You are my reason for choosing to grow over comfort, and to choose purpose over fear.

To the friends who poured wisdom, truth, and encouragement into my life, thank you for reminding me who I was when I forgot.

To every client, mentee, and individual who trusted me with their story, you taught me as I've taught you. Your courage inspired these pages.

And finally, to you, the reader, thank you for choosing growth. Thank you for trusting me on this journey. Thank you for being willing to look inward and rise.

This book is proof that healing is possible, purpose is personal, and success is not accidental.

It is intentional.

It is aligned.

And it is yours.

About the Author

Shez is a qualified transformational coach, CEO, educator, podcast and radio host, author, and founder of a charitable organisation dedicated to empowering individuals to heal, grow, and live with purpose.

Since 2013, she has helped transform the lives of thousands, supporting individuals and marginalised communities to break cycles, overcome trauma, and build sustainable success through faith, mindset, and intentional action.

Her work is rooted in lived experience.

Raised by her grandmother and shaped by adversity, she knows the challenges of living in survival mode. Shez has seen the power of faith in action; her foundation is discipline and belief.

Her approach combines compassion and accountability, helping people move from surviving to overcoming.

In **Successful U**, Shez challenges conventional definitions of success and invites readers to define it for themselves—not by fame or applause, but by alignment, integrity, and purpose.

True success comes when faith and action unite. Growth becomes a lifestyle, and healing is a choice.

Successful U builds on that foundation, offering a practical framework for transformation that guides readers to stop existing, start leading their lives intentionally, and become the most successful version of themselves.

Through coaching, ministry, business, and charity, Shez is a voice of hope and action for a generation ready to rise, rebuild, and thrive.

Appendix A: 30 Day Health and Being Tracker - Week 1

WEEK 1 — HEALTH AND WELL-BEING CHECK-IN

Week of: ____________________

Day	How am I feeling today? (physically, mentally, emotionally)	What influenced my health or well-being today?	What helped me care for or support myself today?
Sunday			
Monday			
Tuesday			
Wednesday			
Thursday			
Friday			
Saturday			

Appendix A: 30 Day Health and Being Tracker - Week 2

WEEK 2— HEALTH AND WELL-BEING CHECK-IN

Week of: ____________

Day	How am I feeling today? (physically, mentally, emotionally)	What influenced my health or well-being today?	What helped me care for or support myself today?
Sunday			
Monday			
Tuesday			
Wednesday			
Thursday			
Friday			
Saturday			

Appendix A: 30 Day Health and Being Tracker - Week 3

WEEK 3— HEALTH AND WELL-BEING CHECK-IN

Week of: ______

Day	How am I feeling today? (physically, mentally, emotionally)	What influenced my health or well-being today?	What helped me care for or support myself today?
Sunday			
Monday			
Tuesday			
Wednesday			
Thursday			
Friday			
Saturday			

Appendix A: 30 Day Health and Being Tracker - Week 4

WEEK 4— HEALTH AND WELL-BEING CHECK-IN

Week of: ____________

Day	How am I feeling today? (physically, mentally, emotionally)	What influenced my health or well-being today?	What helped me care for or support myself today?
Sunday			
Monday			
Tuesday			
Wednesday			
Thursday			
Friday			
Saturday			

Appendix A: 30 Day Health and Being Tracker - Week 5

WEEK 5— HEALTH AND WELL-BEING CHECK-IN

Week of: ____________________

Day	How am I feeling today? (physically, mentally, emotionally)	What influenced my health or well-being today?	What helped me care for or support myself today?
Sunday			
Monday			
Tuesday			
Wednesday			
Thursday			
Friday			
Saturday			

Successful U Self-Assessment

Your Self Evaluation

This assessment is designed to help you honestly evaluate where you are right now in your transformation journey. It's not about perfection—it's about awareness. By identifying which areas you've already begun to master and which ones need more attention, you can create a focused action plan that meets you exactly where you are.

Take your time. Be honest. This is between you and the person you're becoming.

Section 1: The Power of the Mind

Rate yourself honestly on a scale of 1-5

(1 = Not at all true, 5 = Completely true)

1. I regularly examine my thoughts and challenge negative patterns before they take root. ___
2. I believe that renewing my mind is essential to transforming my life. ___
3. I can identify when my thoughts are holding me back from taking action. ___
4. I actively replace negative self-talk with truth-based affirmations. ___
5. I understand that my mindset directly impacts my out-

comes and relationships. ___

Section 1 Total: _____ / 25

🔓 Section 2: Breaking Limiting Beliefs

Rate yourself honestly on a scale of 1-5
(1 = Not at all true, 5 = Completely true)

1. I can name at least three limiting beliefs that have shaped my decisions in the past. ___
2. I regularly question whether my beliefs about myself are actually true. ___
3. I have replaced at least one major limiting belief with an empowering truth. ___
4. I no longer allow my past failures to define my future possibilities. ___
5. I believe that change is possible for me, regardless of my history. ___

Section 2 Total: _____ / 25

🎯 Section 3: Faith in Motion (Goal Setting)

Rate yourself honestly on a scale of 1-5
(1 = Not at all true, 5 = Completely true)

1. I have a clear, written vision for my life that reflects my values and calling. ___
2. I set SMART goals (Specific, Measurable, Achievable, Relevant, Time-bound) regularly. ___
3. I take consistent action toward my goals, even when I don't feel ready. ___
4. I trust God's timing while still doing my part to move forward. ___
5. I review and adjust my goals regularly to ensure they align with my purpose. ___

Section 3 Total: _____ / 25

💪 Section 4: Resilience and Adaptability

Rate yourself honestly on a scale of 1-5
(1 = Not at all true, 5 = Completely true)

1. I bounce back from setbacks without letting them define me. ___
2. I view challenges as opportunities for growth rather than reasons to quit. ___
3. I have healthy coping strategies that help me manage stress and disappointment. ___
4. I can adapt my plans when circumstances change without losing sight of my vision. ___
5. I believe that my past pain has equipped me with strength for my future. ___

Section 4 Total: _____ / 25

🌿 Section 5: Health and Well-Being

Rate yourself honestly on a scale of 1-5
(1 = Not at all true, 5 = Completely true)

1. I prioritise my physical health through regular movement and nourishing food. ___

2. I practice stress management techniques and give myself permission to rest. ___

3. I recognise the warning signs when my body or mind needs attention. ___

4. I understand that self-care is not selfish—it's essential for sustainable success. ___

5. I maintain balance across all four pillars: physical, mental, emotional, and spiritual health. ___

Section 5 Total: _____ / 25

🤝 Section 6: Positive Relationships

Rate yourself honestly on a scale of 1-5
(1 = Not at all true, 5 = Completely true)

1. I have identified the people in my life who genuinely support my growth. ___

2. I communicate my needs clearly and set healthy boundaries when necessary. ___

3. I actively invest time and energy into relationships that

align with my values. ___

4. I have distanced myself from toxic relationships or patterns that drain me. ___
5. I practice active listening and show up authentically in my relationships. ___

Section 6 Total: _____ / 25

💰 Section 7: Financial Independence

Rate yourself honestly on a scale of 1-5

(1 = Not at all true, 5 = Completely true)

1. I have examined my beliefs about money and identified any unhealthy patterns. ___
2. I follow a budget and track my income, expenses, and savings regularly. ___
3. I am actively working toward building an emergency fund and reducing debt. ___
4. I understand the basics of investing and have started (or plan to start) investing. ___
5. I view money as a tool for freedom, generosity, and purpose—not as the enemy. ___

Section 7 Total: _____ / 25

📊 Your Total Score

Add up all seven section totals: _____ / 175

🔍 Scoring Guide: What Your Results Mean

140–175 points: Thriving in Transformation
You are actively living out the principles in this book. You've built strong foundations across multiple areas and are experiencing real growth. Keep going—your consistency is paying off. Now focus on mentoring others and deepening the areas where you scored lowest.

105–139 points: Growing with Intention
You're making solid progress and have embraced several key concepts. Some areas are stronger than others, and that's completely normal. Use this assessment to identify where to focus next. You're on the right path—don't stop now.

70–104 points: Building Momentum
You're beginning to see the value of transformation, but there's still work to do. You may be stuck in certain areas or struggling to take consistent action. That's okay—awareness is the first

step. Choose one or two sections with the lowest scores and commit to focused growth there.

35–69 points: Starting the Journey
You're at the beginning, and that takes courage. The fact that you completed this assessment shows you're ready for change. Don't be discouraged by your score—use it as a baseline. Start small: pick one area, reread that chapter, and take one action this week.

Below 35 points: Ready for a Fresh Start
You may feel stuck, overwhelmed, or unsure where to begin. That's exactly why this book exists. Go back to the Introduction and Chapter 1. Focus on renewing your mind first—everything else will follow. Remember: transformation is possible, and it starts with belief.

💭 Reflection Questions

Take a few moments to reflect on your results:

1. Which section did you score highest in?
What has contributed to your strength in this area? How can you use this strength to support growth in other areas?

2. Which section did you score lowest in?

What specific belief, habit, or fear might be holding you back here? What would change if you gave this area focused attention for the next 30 days?

3. What surprised you most about your results?
Did any score feel higher or lower than you expected? What does that reveal about your self-awareness?

4. If you could only focus on ONE area for the next month, which would it be and why?

🚀 Action Steps Based on Your Results

If your lowest score was in "The Power of the Mind" or "Breaking Limiting Beliefs":

- Reread Chapters 1 and 2
- Complete the "Renew Your Mind" exercise daily for 21 days
- Write down three limiting beliefs and replace them with truth-based affirmations
- Find an accountability partner to check in with weekly

If your lowest score was in "Faith in Motion":

- Revisit the Vision to Action Framework in Chapter 3
- Write out your vision and create at least three SMART goals
- Schedule time each week to review your progress
- Take one small action toward your biggest goal this week

If your lowest score was in "Resilience and Adaptability":

- Reread Chapter 4 and journal about a recent setback
- Identify one coping strategy you can practice this week
- Reflect on a past challenge you overcame—what strengths did you use?
- Commit to reframing one negative situation as a growth opportunity

If your lowest score was in "Health and Well-Being":

- Use the 30-Day Health and Wellbeing Tracker in Appendix A

- Choose one pillar (physical, mental, emotional, or spiritual) to focus on first
- Schedule rest and self-care into your calendar like any other appointment
- Identify one boundary you need to set to protect your well-being

If your lowest score was in "Positive Relationships":

- Reread Chapter 6 and list your current relationships in three categories: life-giving, neutral, draining
- Practice setting one small boundary this week
- Reach out to one person who supports your growth
- Reflect on your communication style—are you listening as much as you're speaking?

If your lowest score was in "Financial Independence":

- Reread Chapter 7 and complete the "Money Mindset Reflection" exercise
- Create or review your budget using the 50/30/20 rule
- Open a savings account or set up an automatic transfer to start your emergency fund

- Research one investment option (ISA, index fund, etc.) and commit to learning more

🌱 A Final Word on Growth

This assessment is not a one-time snapshot—it's a tool you can return to again and again. I encourage you to retake it every 90 days as you continue your journey. You'll be amazed at how much you grow when you're intentional about it.

Remember: low scores are not failures. They're simply invitations to grow. High scores are not finish lines. They're reminders to keep going and to help others along the way.

Transformation is not about perfection. It's about progression.

You are not the same person who started reading this book. And six months from now, you'll look back at today's score and see just how far you've come.

Keep going. Keep growing. Keep becoming.

You are already on your way to becoming *Successful U.*

📖 Glossary of Terms

Financial Terms

50/30/20 Rule: A budgeting method that allocates 50% of income to needs, 30% to wants, and 20% to savings and debt repayment. This approach helps create financial balance and intentional spending.

Compound Interest: The process where interest is earned not just on the original investment, but also on the accumulated interest over time. It's often described as "earning interest on your interest," allowing money to grow exponentially.

Dividend Stocks: Shares in companies that regularly distribute a portion of their earnings to shareholders. These provide a potential source of passive income and can be part of a diversified investment strategy.

Emergency Fund: A financial safety net of liquid savings typically covering 3-6 months of living expenses. This fund provides financial security during unexpected life events like job loss or medical emergencies.

Financial Independence: The state of having sufficient personal wealth and resources to live without actively working for basic necessities. It represents the freedom to make life choices without being primarily constrained by financial limitations.

Index Funds: Investment funds that track a specific market index, offering broad market exposure with lower fees compared to actively managed funds. They provide a simple way to diversify investments.

Passive Income: Earnings generated with minimal ongoing effort, such as rental income, royalties, or investment returns. This income stream can provide financial flexibility and reduce dependence on traditional employment.

Peer-to-Peer Lending: An alternative financial model where individuals can lend and borrow money directly through online platforms, bypassing traditional banking institutions.

Roth IRA: A retirement savings account where contributions are made with after-tax dollars, allowing tax-free withdrawals during retirement. (UK equivalent: Stocks and Shares ISA)

Goal-Setting & Personal Development Terms

Alignment: The process of harmonizing personal values, actions, and goals to create a coherent and authentic life path. It involves ensuring that daily choices reflect core beliefs and long-term objectives.

Closed/Fixed Mindset: A belief that personal qualities and abilities are static and unchangeable. People with this mindset tend to avoid challenges and see effort as fruitless.

Goals (SMART): A goal-setting framework where objectives are

Specific, Measurable, Achievable, Relevant, and Time-bound. This approach increases the likelihood of successful goal achievement.

Growth Mindset: The belief that abilities and intelligence can be developed through dedication, learning, and persistent effort. It embraces challenges as opportunities for personal development.

Integrity: Consistently adhering to strong ethical principles and being true to one's values, even when it's challenging or potentially disadvantageous.

Purpose: The deeper reason behind one's actions and life choices, transcending immediate goals and connecting to a broader sense of meaning and contribution.

Vision: A clear, inspiring mental image of a desired future state or outcome. It serves as a guiding principle for personal and professional development.

Health & Wellness Terms

Active Listening: A communication technique involving fully concentrating, understanding, responding, and remembering what is being said. It demonstrates respect and deepens interpersonal connections.

Amygdala: A part of the brain responsible for processing emotions, particularly fear and stress responses. It plays a crucial role in the body's fight-or-flight mechanism.

Boundaries: Personal guidelines that define acceptable behaviour from others and help protect emotional and mental well-being. They communicate individual needs and limits clearly.

Burnout: A state of emotional, physical, and mental exhaustion caused by prolonged stress, often resulting from overwhelming work or personal responsibilities.

Holistic Life Advantage™ Framework: An integrated approach to personal development that considers physical, mental, emotional, and spiritual dimensions of well-being.

Limiting Beliefs: Negative, often unconscious thoughts that constrain an individual's potential and prevent personal growth. These beliefs typically stem from past experiences and can significantly impact decision-making.

Resilience: The capacity to recover quickly from difficulties, adapt to challenges, and bounce back from setbacks. It involves maintaining mental and emotional strength during adversity.

Stewardship: Responsible management and care of resources, including personal talents, time, finances, and relationships, with a focus on long-term sustainability and positive impact.

Glossary of Terms

www.ingramcontent.com/pod-product-compliance
Lightning Source LLC
LaVergne TN
LVHW020510100826
845148LV00003B/745
9798902432883